A
GUIDE TO GROWING
THE APPLE

WITH INFORMATION ON SOIL, TREE FORMS,
ROOTSTOCKS, PESTS, VARIETIES AND MUCH
MORE

BY
N. BAGENAL

British Library Cataloguing-in-Publication Data

A catalogue record for this book is available from the
British Library

CONTENTS

Introduction to Fruit Growing

In botany, a fruit is a part of a flowering plant that derives from specific tissues of the flower, one or more ovaries, and in some cases accessory tissues. In common language use though, 'fruit' normally means the fleshy seed-associated structures of a plant that are sweet or sour, and edible in the raw state, such as apples, oranges, grapes, strawberries, bananas, and lemons. Many fruit bearing plants have grown alongside the movements of humans and animals in a symbiotic relationship, as a means for seed dispersal and nutrition respectively. In fact, humans and many animals have become dependent on fruits as a source of food. Fruits account for a substantial fraction of the world's agricultural output, and some (such as the apple and the pomegranate) have acquired extensive cultural and symbolic meanings. Today, most fruit is produced using traditional farming practices, in large orchards or plantations, utilising pesticides and often the employment of hundreds of workers. However, the yield of fruit from organic farming is growing – and, importantly, many individuals are starting to grow their own fruits and vegetables. This historic and incredibly important foodstuff is gradually making a come-back into the individual garden.

The scientific study and cultivation of fruits is called 'pomology', and this branch of methodology divides fruits into groups based on plant morphology and anatomy. Some of these useful subdivisions broadly incorporate 'Pome Fruits', including apples and pears, and 'Stone Fruits' so called because of their characteristic middle, including peaches, almonds, apricots, plums and cherries. Many hundreds of fruits, including fleshy fruits like apple, peach, pear, kiwifruit, watermelon and mango are commercially valuable as human food, eaten both fresh and as jams, marmalade and other preserves, as well as in other recipes. Because fruits have been such a major part of the human diet, different cultures have developed many varying uses for fruits, which often do not revolve around eating. Many dry fruits are used as decorations or in dried flower arrangements, such as lotus, wheat, annual honesty and milkweed, whilst ornamental trees and shrubs are often cultivated for their colourful fruits (including holly, pyracantha, viburnum, skimmia, beautyberry and cotoneaster).

These widespread uses, practical as well as edible, make fruits a perfect thing to grow at home; and dependent on location and climate – they can be very low-maintenance crops. One of the most common fruits found in the British countryside (and towns for that matter) is the blackberry bush, which thrives in most soils – apart from those which are poorly drained or mostly made of dry or sandy soil. Apple trees are, of course, are another classic and whilst they may take several years to grow into a well-established tree, they will grow nicely in most sunny and well composted areas. Growing one's own fresh, juicy tomatoes is one of the great pleasures of summer gardening, and even if the gardener doesn't have room for rows of plants, pots or hanging baskets are a fantastic solution. The types, methods and approaches to growing fruit are myriad, and far too numerous to be discussed in any detail here, but there are always easy ways to get started for the complete novice. We hope that the reader is inspired by this book on fruit and fruit growing – and is encouraged to start, or continue their own cultivations. Good Luck!

THE APPLE
(Pyrus Malus)

ORIGIN AND HISTORY

Apples appear to have been grown in England from the earliest times. For centuries they were used mainly for the making of cider, but with the introduction from the Continent of new varieties under the patronage of the Church, the Crown and the nobility, the apple gradually came to be regarded as a garden and orchard tree, until to-day it is more widely grown in England than any other fruit.

SOIL, SITUATION AND ASPECT

Apple trees can be grown successfully on a wide range of soil series. Those that are badly drained and liable to waterlogging at any depth down to three or four feet should be avoided, as also should those which are excessively drained and liable to dry out in a hot summer. Soils with a high nitrogen content such as are to be found in old hop gardens or in heavily-manured kitchen gardens, should not be used for planting apples until means has been found to reduce the amount of nitrogen that is available to the young trees.

If apples must be planted under high nitrogen conditions, cooking apples should be selected in preference to dessert varieties.

Sandy soils are usually deficient in potassium, and apple

trees planted under these conditions will always need generous manuring with sulphate of potash. Shelter from the south-west and from the east winds and protection from spring frosts are necessary for successful apple culture. Although the apple can be grown under conditions of moderately high rainfall and low sunshine, these are by no means ideal conditions. It would appear that good dessert apples are grown most economically in districts with a yearly rainfall of from 20 to 25 inches, and with a correspondingly high rate of sunshine, these being conditions which impose a natural check on excessive growth, and ensure good skin colour and texture in the fruit. This does not mean that good dessert apples cannot be grown under conditions of medium to high rainfall, but that greater skill is required to produce the same results.

In districts of more than 40 inches of rainfall in the year, dessert apples must be regarded as difficult to grow successfully, and preference should be given to cooking apples.

FORM OF TREE

The form of tree to be adopted must be considered in relation to the type of apple culture required.

Grass Orchards.—For grass orchards where stock is grazing, the standard, three-quarter-standard and half-standard forms may be used according to the height above the ground at which it is necessary to keep the branches out of reach of grazing stock. Where there is no grazing stock, the bush form may be used in a grass orchard quite as well as the standards, and is to be preferred because it is more economical to prune, spray, thin and pick. It does not necessarily follow that a fruit tree grown in the form of a bush must necessarily be of small or medium size, since it is not the form of a tree but the rootstock, the variety and the subsequent management which ultimately determine its size. In actual fact, the standard forms are usually larger than others because the trees are on the most vigorous rootstocks, but it is possible to produce bush trees of any size according to the purpose for which they are required.

Commercial Plantations.—For commercial plantations the bush form is the most popular and is used in all sizes from the very large "permanent" to the very small "filler."

The oblique cordon form has been largely used for intensive apple culture, and in more recent years, the double cordon, the dwarf pyramid or dwarf fuseau forms have all been planted.

The Fruit Garden.—For the fruit garden there are several forms of apple tree to suit the space available. Where there is very little headroom and hardly any lateral space in more than two directions, the horizontal cordon may be used, the trees being planted at intervals of from 10 to 12 feet for subsequent inarch grafting of one into the other. Where there is headroom but only limited lateral space in more than two directions, the vertical cordon, either single or double, the oblique cordon, and the espalier forms all have their peculiar merits. Where both headroom and lateral space in all directions are limited, the dwarf pyramid and bush forms may be useful, and where there are no restrictions of space, the large bush and even the half-standard may be used with advantage.

ROOTSTOCKS FOR APPLES

Apple trees are raised by budding or grafting the scion variety (see pages 41–52) on to a rootstock raised either vegetatively by stooling and layering or from seed (see pages 37–40). The advantage of using vegetatively-raised rootstocks for fruit trees lies in the fact that the stocks from any one stool or layer can be depended upon to produce the same type of tree, and the same type of fruit in the scion variety. This uniformity makes it easier to control the behaviour of the individual trees than it would be if they were worked on different seedling rootstocks. For Vegetative Propagation by Layering, see Rootstocks, page 39.

SELECTION OF ROOTSTOCKS

Before grafting or budding a tree, or when ordering trees ready-worked, careful consideration should be given to the selection of the most suitable rootstock. Research has shown that the size of the tree when fully grown and, to a certain extent, the quality of the fruit are influenced by the rootstock. Local conditions, particularly the nature of the soil, should also be borne in mind when selecting the rootstock. For instance, if the conditions are conducive to excessive growth, the stock chosen should be of a more dwarfing nature than would normally be required for the purpose, and vice versa. In the light of present knowledge the most useful standardized apple rootstocks for different sizes of tree are as follows:—

Rootstocks for Dwarf Trees

Jaune de Metz (also called Malling Number Nine).—Under favourable growth conditions this stock makes a small but healthy tree which begins to come into bearing in from two to three years' time, and which throughout its life remains smaller than on any other commercial rootstock. Number Nine has recently fallen into disfavour with some commercial fruit-growers, partly because its roots are brittle and the trees are, therefore, liable to be blown over in a storm unless carefully staked, and partly because, unless the trees are planted under favourable growth conditions and carefully nursed when young, they are apt to make rather poor trees.

On the other hand, the early cropping of trees on this stock, combined with the high colour and large size of fruit which it tends to produce in trees worked upon it, make Number Nine the ideal rootstock for all varieties of apples grown under garden conditions. Here the natural shelter and the artificial support afforded by wall, fence, or wire can be relied upon to prevent the trees from being blown over.

Rootstocks for Trees of Medium Size

Doucin (Malling Number Two) and *Broadleaf* (Mailing Number One).—At the present time the stock which appears to be most widely used by English nurserymen for bush trees, and which is also being used for cordons in many commercial plantations, is the Doucin (called Mailing Number Two). In early years this is a semi-dwarfing stock with all Varieties, but with *Cox's Orange Pippin* and some other sorts it becomes more vigorous as the trees grow older. The Broadleaf (also called Mailing Number One) is a stock which appears to be more vigorous with some varieties than with others. *Cox's Orange Pippin* on Number One starts off fairly strongly and then settles down into a semi-dwarf tree, whereas with *Worcester Pearmain* and *Bramley's Seedling* there appears to be little to choose in size in later years between trees on Numbers One and Two. At East Mailing Research Station, Number One has given a rather brighter colour to dessert apples such as *Worcester Pearmain* than Number Two. From the experimental point of view, it is not yet possible to say which of these two rootstocks is the better for commercial cordon plantations. Number Nine is the most suitable stock for *Cox's Orange Pippin* Cordons.

Rootstocks for Very Large Trees

Mailing Number Twelve and Number Sixteen.—Of the standardized rootstocks for very large trees, whether standard, three-quarter-standard, half-standard or bush, Mailing

Numbers Twelve and Sixteen are to be recommended, trees on Number Twelve taking rather longer to come into bearing than those on Number Sixteen. Failing this, the trees should be on selected free or crab stocks, such as Mailing Crab C., or one of the Long Ashton selections.

PRUNING OF APPLES

The general principles of pruning have been dealt with in Chapter V (Pruning), where it was pointed out that winter and summer pruning are two very different operations and affect the tree in different ways. In theory true "winter" pruning should be done only when the tree is in its most dormant stage, i.e., when there is the minimum flow of sap upwards or downwards. In practice there appears to be a fairly wide margin of time on either side of this stage when winter pruning may safely be carried out, without making any appreciable difference to the results. On very large fruit farms winter pruning often starts before leaf-fall in the autumn, and if bad weather intervenes, it may not be finished until just before bud-break. Probably the second half of November and December form the optimum period for winter pruning, and whenever possible, it should be completed before winter washing begins, if only to economize in the amount of spray required.

Very strong-growing varieties of apple, such as *Bramley's Seedling*, need little winter pruning after the first few years, the main object in such cases being to keep the centre of the tree fairly open, by spurring back ingrowing laterals, and cutting out interlacing branches.

One of the main difficulties with such varieties on vigorous stocks is to get the tree to come into bearing, and since hard winter pruning is one of the chief factors in delaying cropping, it follows that the less pruning such trees receive in early years the more quickly they will crop. Nothing is more fatal to quick cropping than the old-fashioned method of pruning the leading shoots and all laterals hard back every winter before the tree has come into bearing. If the leaders are only lightly tipped or even left entirely unpruned after, say, the third or fourth year from planting, and all the laterals of medium growth on the outside of the tree are left full length for one or two seasons, the trees will come into bearing reasonably quickly. If this is not done, strong growers like *Bramley's Seedling* and varieties like *Allington Pippin* and *Cox's Orange*, which make much lateral growth, may go on growing vigorously without cropping for years after they should have come into bearing.

Another varietal habit which is important in determining the degree of winter pruning for apples is the way in which the tree naturally carries its fruit-buds. Some varieties, such as *Worcester Pearmain, Bismarck, Gladstone, Grenadier, Irish Peach, Barnack Beauty, Cornish Gillyflower, St. Edmund's Russet*, and to a certain extent *Bramley's Seedling*, are what are known as "tip-bearers," carrying their fruit-buds, especially in early years, at the end of rather thin, twiggy lateral shoots. If these laterals are cut hard back in winter to within a few inches of the base, the fruit-buds are all cut away and the trees cannot be expected to bear fruit. To be fruitful such laterals must be left full length and allowed rather an untidy appearance in early years. (See Illustration facing page 65.)

Other varieties, such as *James Grieve, Cox's Orange Pippin, Early Victoria, Egremont Russet, Ribston Pippin, Lord Derby, Edward VII, Miller's Seedling* and *Duchess Favourite,* carry a large proportion of their fruit-buds on naturally-formed fruit-spurs or on artificial spurs made by shortening back the lateral shoots. Such varieties are naturally much easier to spur-prune than tip-bearers, and can be made to look tidy without ruining their prospect of cropping, provided always the leaders are not pruned too hard during the critical period in which the trees are coming into bearing. (See Illustration facing page 65.)

The more artificial the form of the tree, the more difficult it is to lay down hard and fast rules for successful pruning. With the standard and the bush forms the vegetative vigour of the tree can be distributed in lateral shoots over a large number of main branches, but when it comes to limiting the main branches to one, two, three or even to ten main branches as in cordons, pyramids, fuseaux and espaliers, there will always be the problem of how to deal with the dense crop of closely-growing new laterals which in the more natural forms of tree have room to spread themselves without overcrowding. With such trees the first essential is to leave the leaders as long as possible in order to counteract the tendency to throw out strong new shoots immediately behind them. Late spring pruning of the leader, when about one inch of new growth has already been made, will prove an additional check to this unwanted vegetative vigour, but probably the most certain method for all these artificial forms of tree is to adopt one or other of the summer pruning treatments already described in Chapter V.

Apples of Upright Habit of Growth.	Apples of Spreading Habit of Growth.	Varieties that Need to be Pruned lightly.
Adam's Pearmain	Belle de Boskoop	Blenheim Orange
Annie Elizabeth	Blenheim Orange	Bramley's Seedling
Christmas Pearmain	Bramley's Seedling	Belle de Boskoop
Edward VII	Gladstone	
Egremont Russet	Lane's Prince Albert	
Heusgen's Golden Reinette	Langley Pippin	
John Standish	Stirling Castle	
King of the Pippins		
Lord Derby		
Orleans Reinette		
Worcester Pearmain		

There is a certain amount of empirical evidence to show that when summer pruning shoots in a semi-woody condition back to about 5 or 6 inches, if the shoots are merely broken or "brutted," and allowed to hang down without being severed, there is less likelihood of secondary growth taking place than if the shoots were cut cleanly through with a knife or secateurs. "Brutting" is a common practice in the summer pruning of

Kentish cobnuts, and although it gives the tree an untidy appearance, it may help to check the tendency to excessive lateral growth in cordons, espaliers and other artificial forms.

Whether summer pruned or not, new lateral shoots (with the exception of tip-bearers) are usually pruned or "spurred" back at the end of the first season's growth to 3, 4 or 5 inches from the base according to their strength (page 57). The stronger the lateral within limits, the more lightly it should be pruned. During the following season it is quite likely that one or more woodbuds on this spurred lateral may send out shoots of varying length, and that one or even two buds toward the base will swell out and begin to look as if they might be fruit-buds. It is advisable not to cut hard back to these buds the following winter, but to cut back the new laterals on the old spur to within from 1/2 inch to 2 inches of their base according to their vigour.

It has been found by experiment that better results are obtained by allowing fruit-buds to form gradually on these artificial spurs rather than by stimulating them into growth by cutting hard back to them the first year. When there is no longer any doubt that fruit-buds are present at the base of the spur, the lateral shoots above them can be safely cut back to the fruit-spur.

For an account of "Delayed Open-Centre" Pruning, see Chapter VII.

MANURING OF APPLES

Potassium.—In Chapter III attention was drawn to the fact that in this country potassium is the most important fertilizer for apples.

Symptoms of Potassium Deficiency.—The chief symptoms of potash deficiency in the apple, as in other fruit trees and bushes, is a marginal browning of the leaf known as "leaf-scorch." This is not invariably a sign of lack of potash, there being other causes such as severe drought, or spray-damage which may cause scorching of the leaf. When, however, there is reason to suspect a deficiency of potassium available to the tree and "scorch" is prevalent on the margins of the leaf, the "immediate action" is to apply potash. Experiments have shown that sulphate of potash is the most satisfactory form in which to apply potassium to the soil for apple trees, in amounts varying from 2 to 4 cwt. per acre (1 to 2 oz. per square yard). In cases of acute potassium deficiency as much as 8 cwt. per acre (equal to 1/2 lb. per square yard) has been applied.

Nitrogen.—Young apple trees are usually better without nitrogenous manures. For trees in bearing the quantity required depends on the kind, variety and growth-conditions of the tree. For instance, cooking apples will take more nitrogen than dessert apples, and among dessert apples *Cox's Orange Pippin* will take more than *Worcester Pearmain*.

Symptoms of Excess Nitrogen.—Much vigorous shoot growth,

very large, dark green leaves, badly-coloured fruit of greasy texture and poor keeping quality, and susceptibility to attack by the canker fungus, all these are symptoms of excess nitrogen in the apple tree. Trees showing such symptoms should receive no nitrogenous manures, and cultivations should be stopped altogether or limited to the first half of the growing season. Other alternatives are to leave the trees entirely unpruned, and in extreme cases to ring-bark or even to root-prune.

Symptoms of Nitrogen Deficiency.—Small weak shoots, small pale green leaves, small, sweet, highly-coloured fruit of good texture and good keeping quality, these are the symptoms of nitrogen shortage in the apple tree. The high colour of the fruit and the good keeping quality are both desirable conditions in dessert apples, and where these are required the less nitrogen the trees get the better, so long as the leaf does not get too small and yellow and provided the trees are not allowed to stop growing altogether. When this happens, it is often better, before applying nitrogen, to try the effect of one or more of the other growth-promoting measures, such as thorough cultivations or hard pruning. Trees on weak stocks may be invigorated by planting one or more vigorous rootstocks close beside the tree and inarching them into the stem below the bottom branches. Trees which are deficient both in nitrogen and in potassium will require heavy feeding with potash before they can benefit from applications of nitrogenous manures.

Forms and Amounts of Nitrogen for Apple Trees.—Of the

organic forms of manure, farmyard dung, high-grade shoddy, and meat and bonemeal are most widely used by commercial growers for supplying nitrogen to apple trees. The organic forms are generally used on light soils to keep the moisture in the ground during the summer months.

Of the inorganic forms of nitrogenous fertilizer, sulphate of ammonia, nitrate of soda, and nitro-chalk are the most popular and are given usually in two half-dressings, say in February and May. Strong-growing varieties of cooking apples, such as *Bramley's Seedling* when in full bearing, may require up to 5 cwt. per acre, or even more, to give healthy foliage and large-sized fruits, provided the potash applications are being well-maintained. Dessert apples like *Cox's Orange Pippin*, on the other hand, even when in full bearing, should not require more than half this amount. In the light of present knowledge it is not possible to prescribe the exact amounts of nitrogen and potassium to apply. The trees themselves are the most reliable indicators of their own needs, and the wise fruit-grower will look to them for guidance.

Phosphorus.—Field experiments have so far failed to show exactly in what way, if any, phosphorus is necessary for an apple tree in this country. At the same time, many successful fruit-growers emphasize the importance of this element, and until experiments prove it to be unnecessary, experts are agreed in recommending the application of some form of phosphatic manure to apple trees. Steamed bone flour, is, perhaps, the most popular of the organic forms, and superphosphates and basic slag are both used as inorganic forms. Rates of application vary, 5 cwt. per acre being about the average dressing, applied in winter or very early spring.

Magnesium.—See page 35.

GUIDE TO THE MANURING OF APPLE TREES

The following table indicates the conditions under which the requirements of the trees for Potassium (K) and Nitrogen (N) are likely to be either more or less than normal.

	Subsoil Sandy, Gravelly or Badly-drained	Hard Pruned	Light Pruned	Cooking Apple	Dessert Apple	Uncultivated (Grass or Weeds)	Cultivated (No weeds or grass)
Potassium (K) ...	More	More	Less	Less	More	Less	More
Nitrogen (N) ...	More	Less	More	More	Less	More	Less

INDICATIONS OF MANURIAL REQUIREMENTS

Symptoms	Probable Cause
Leaves, marginal browning, "Leaf-scorch"	Potash deficiency
Leaves, large and dark green, vigorous shoot growth; badly-coloured fruit of greasy texture and poor keeping quality	Excess of Nitrogen
Leaves, small and pale green, weak shoots; small, highly-coloured, sweet fruit of good texture and good keeping quality	Nitrogen deficiency

FRUIT THINNING

The three main objects in fruit thinning are to increase the ultimate size of the fruits which remain, to give a uniform sample, and to induce regular bearing in the tree. There is no doubt that with the codling types of apple, such as *Lord Suffield, Lord Grosvenor, Keswick Codling* and *Early Victoria (Emneth Early)*, thinning the fruits to 8 or 10 inches apart when they are the size of walnuts is much the best way to get large fruit. The same is true of varieties like *Miller's Seedling, Duchess Favourite*, and *John Standish*, which normally produce rather small-sized apples.

It is becoming a widespread practice among commercial fruitgrowers to thin dessert apples such as *Worcester Pearmain* and *Cox's Orange Pippin*, leaving not more than two, and often only one fruit to a truss, with a view to getting uniformity of size in the fruit. When thinning, the centre fruit of each truss, the "King" apple, is removed, because it is usually an abnormal fruit, which is often misshapen, and does not always keep well in store.

The best way to thin apples is to take the stalk between the first and second fingers of the right hand and to push the apple gently but firmly off its stalk with the thumb of the same hand.

GATHERING OF FRUIT

Different varieties of apples ripen in different months. Early ripening varieties should be picked over more than once, and cannot be kept for more than a few weeks except in low-temperature stores. Keeping varieties of apple develop more slowly, and late colouring varieties, if they are to be really well coloured, ought to be left on the tree as long as possible. It is generally considered that one of the best tests of whether an apple is ready for picking is to lift it gently on its stalk. If the apple comes away without an effort, the fruit is usually sufficiently ripe to finish the rest of the ripening process off the tree. If it is picked at a stage when the stalk has to be torn off, there is a likelihood that the apple may not keep well in ordinary storage. It should be emphasized, however, that for low-temperature storage of any kind, the fruit is best picked rather sooner than it would be for ordinary storage.

For selections of *Early, Mid-season* and *Late* varieties, see page 192.

Weather for Gathering.—Apples should be gathered when they are quite dry and should not be exposed unnecessarily to the sun after being picked.

For *Storing, Marketing* and *Exhibiting*, see pages 108–118.

INSECT PESTS OF THE APPLE

Apples are liable to attack by more pests than any other fruit crop, and this accounts for the large Spray Schedule for apples given on page 142.

WINTER MOTHS

In the spring the opening buds are attacked by caterpillars of the Winter Moth. These are at first very small and dark coloured, but eventually become an inch or more in length, green in colour, and may always be recognized by their characteristic "looping" method of walking. When small they feed in the buds and blossom trusses, but when foliage becomes more plentiful, they feed on the leaves, and often destroy small fruits also. In very large numbers they can defoliate the trees, with serious consequences. In June they drop to the ground and turn to pupæ (chrysalids) in the soil. Here they remain till winter comes, when the moths emerge and make their way to the branches and twigs. There they lay their small, oval, at first green but later reddish-brown eggs from which the destructive caterpillars ultimately develop.

The March Moth is the latest of the several species of winter moth to emerge in the spring. It differs from the others in its habit of laying its full complement of eggs not singly but in a band around a twig.

Control.—Although the male moths can fly readily, the females have no proper wings, and are therefore obliged to crawl up the trunks of the trees. Attack by caterpillars of this type of moth can therefore be prevented by applying grease-bands to the tree trunks in October, and by ensuring that the "tackiness" of the grease is maintained till the spring. If grease-banding is not practised, the trees should be sprayed with lead arsenate when the caterpillars start to appear in April and May.

TORTRIX MOTHS

Tortrix caterpillars can always be recognized by their habit of wriggling backwards when disturbed, and by the way in which they spin the leaves together. Several closely-related species occur, some of which hibernate as tiny caterpillars encased in cocoons of silk and rubbish, which they construct in crevices and under loose bark. From these hiding places they emerge when the buds break and quickly eat their way into the buds, which then wilt or shrivel and turn brown. At this time the caterpillars are still very small, little more than one-tenth of an inch long, and are brown or green or yellowish-green in colour. Later, they feed on the leaves, which they spin together for protection, and, in May or June, turn to pupae or chrysalids which shortly produce moths. These lay minute, pale green, almost colourless eggs on the leaves, either singly or in clusters. About the middle of July more caterpillars hatch out and feed on the leaves and frequently on the fruit too. Small portions of the skin of the apple are eaten but the damage often passes unnoticed when the fruit is picked. Consequently the caterpillars may be introduced into the fruit store, where they continue their feeding. Rotting follows and soon spreads to neighbouring sound apples.

Control.—No one remedy as yet seems adequate for the control of these destructive caterpillars. They can be kept within reasonable limits by the various spray mixtures used for other pests in the normal routine spray schedule (see page 142). Tar-oil winter washes destroy the more accessible of the hibernating larvae, and the lead arsenate applied before, and in some cases after, blossoming destroys many of them whilst they are feeding. Lead arsenate cannot, of course, be safely applied in mid-July; for the fruit-eating generation, therefore, mid-July sprays of non-poisonous materials such as Denis Root should be used.

GREENFLY

Several species of aphides (green- or blackfly) occur on apple trees, and when plentiful can cause severe injury in the form of crippled growth or loss of crop. The two commonest species, the Permanent Green Apple Aphis *(Aphis pomi)* and the Rosy Aphis or Blue Bug *(Anuraphis roseus)*, both spend the winter on the trees as small, black, shiny eggs. The eggs of the former are laid thickly clustered together on the young sappy shoots, whilst those of the Rosy Aphis are laid singly, mainly on the spurs.

The *Green Aphis* hatches in April, when the buds are breaking, but does little damage until June, when it becomes abundant on the younger growths. These become stunted and malformed and often die back from the tip.

The *Rosy Aphis* is a larger insect than the Green Aphis and may be distinguished by its bluish or purple colour and by its mealy appearance. It causes more damage than any other apple aphis, feeding not only on the leaves and shoots, but on the newly-formed fruits also. Badly-affected fruits may drop off altogether; those remaining on the tree become stunted and deformed, especially at the eye end, which becomes "knobbly." In July this insect migrates to certain weeds, such as plantain, but returns to the apple in the autumn.

Owing to their habit of curling the leaves on which they feed, aphides are not always completely destroyed by spring or summer spraying with nicotine. The eggs are easily destroyed by winter tar-oil washes.

WOOLLY APHIS OR AMERICAN BLIGHT
(Eriosoma lanigerum)

This is a severe pest in the nursery and is often troublesome, though of less economic importance, on established trees. The insect itself is reddish in colour, but produces masses of white wax, the "wool," which in bad cases often hangs in festoons from the branches. A few aphides spend the winter on the trunk or main branches, in the shelter of cracks or crevices, and further protected by their covering of wool. In the spring they produce living young, which reproduce rapidly and so give rise to the heavy infestations often experienced in early summer. The insects are spread from tree to tree by the wind, or partly by the wind and partly by crawling over the ground.

The feeding of Woolly Aphis causes gall-like swellings on the twigs and branches. Badly-attacked twigs often die; in any case the galls enlarge and split and become cankerous or provide a ready entrance for the troublesome fungus disease "Apple Canker."

There has been a great deal of controversy as to whether this pest feeds on the roots of apple trees, and it now seems certain that it does not do this to any extent, in this country at any rate.

Control.—If Woolly Aphis is present when the trees are lifted from the nursery they should be dipped in a 10 per cent, solution of tar-oil wash. In the nursery the pest can be kept within bounds by painting the larger colonies with methylated spirit, and by spraying thoroughly with nicotine and soap. Larger trees should, if necessary, also be sprayed with nicotine. This is best applied with the petal-fall scab spray. Winter application of tar-oil wash also helps to keep Woolly

Aphis in check. Should it become troublesome in summer it can be dealt with by means of nicotine, used in conjunction with plenty of soap or with a summer-oil emulsion.

APPLE BLOSSOM WEEVIL
(Anthonomus pomorum)

Very soon after the Winter Moth and Tortrix caterpillars start their damage, the Apple Blossom Weevil emerges from the litter, loose bark or other rubbish in which it has sheltered during the winter, and begins to feed on the buds. This insect is about an eighth of an inch or more in length, grey or black in colour, with a silvery V-shaped mark on its back. It is more or less oval in shape and possesses a long, slightly curved snout or rostrum, the apex of which is furnished with small, powerful jaws. It feeds on the sides of the buds, making small, round holes in the still folded leaves. The chief damage, however, is caused by the grub, which hatches in April from an egg laid within the flower-bud. On hatching it feeds on the stamens and style, sticking the petals down to form a kind of tent above it. Affected blossoms never open but remain "capped" until the petals turn brown and drop off. Such blossoms cannot be pollinated and so are usually unable to set fruit. The grub, which is white and legless and has a black head, develops into a yellow chrysalis and, subsequently, into an adult beetle. In this form it leaves the capped blossom and, after feeding for a while on the leaves and fruits, seeks out suitable sleeping quarters in which to remain till the following spring.

Control.—Sprays have proved of very little use against this pest, but some good can be done by trapping the beetles in sacking or corrugated cardboard bands. These should be placed around the tree trunk in June and removed and burnt in the winter.

APPLE SUCKER
(Psylla mali)

This was formerly one of the most destructive apple pests. Since the advent of tar-oil winter washes, however, it has practically disappeared and is now found chiefly in gardens and neglected plantations. The damage is caused largely by the young insects (nymphs), which hatch out as soon as the buds break, from the very small, yellow, cigar-shaped eggs, which are laid on the spurs and smaller branches in the autumn. The nymph somewhat resembles greenfly, to which it is closely related, but may be distinguished by its flatter shape and more prominent eyes. It is at first minute and yellow, later becoming pale green. The young suckers, which may occur in large numbers, creep into the opening buds and suck the sap. Badly-attacked buds turn brown and fail to grow out, or the blossom may appear and then shrivel and drop off. Sucker damage has often been attributed to frost, but can always be recognized from the drops of white, sticky wax which exude from the suckers. The adult insect is rather more than a tenth of an inch long and possesses transparent wings, which are held roof-like over its back when not in use.

Control.—Sucker eggs can be easily destroyed in winter by means of a tar-oil wash. If this is not done and Sucker appears in the spring, recourse must be had to nicotine, which may be added to one of the pre-blossom scab sprays. (See Guide to Spraying, page 142.)

APPLE CAPSID BUG
(Plesiocoris rugicollis)

When the leaves of the blossom trusses have unfolded, and the green flower buds are visible, the young of the Apple Capsid begin to hatch out. They are very small and green and somewhat resemble greenfly in appearance. Unlike these insects, however, they are very active and at the least alarm run rapidly and hide under a leaf or at the base of the flower-stalks. Capsid bugs feed on both leaves and fruits, first piercing the tissue with their needle-like stylets, and then pumping in salivary juices to enable them to suck up partially-digested sap. Certain toxic materials contained in the salivary juices cause the death of the punctured cells and surrounding tissue.

The first signs of Capsid damage are small black marks, later becoming brown and eventually turning into holes, on the young leaves. Soon after the fruits are set, the bugs feed upon them, the ultimate result frequently being small, deformed fruits disfigured with corky scars. As the Capsid bugs grow in size, they gradually acquire wing pads, fully-developed wings appearing only at the final moult. The winged, adult insects fly from tree to tree, laying their small, elongated eggs beneath the rind of the twigs and branches. Some damage is done by these adult bugs, which feed on the succulent new shoots, producing corky scars and sometimes distorting or even killing the shoots.

Control.—It is essential to destroy the bugs before they begin their attack on the fruits, as they are more easily killed when they are very small. Thorough spraying with nicotine just before the blossom opens will be found effective, especially if spraying is carried out in hot weather. As an alternative, good results can be obtained by using petroleum-oil sprays during the winter or at any time up to bud-break. The type that contains dinitro-cresol obviates the need for prior spraying with tar-oil wash and will deal with the eggs of Sucker and Greenfly as well as those of Capsid.

APPLE SAWFLY

(Hoplocampa testudinea)

This insect makes its appearance when the trees are in bloom, and feeds on the flower pollen prior to laying its eggs.

The adult sawfly is rather more than a quarter of an inch in length, with transparent wings, a conspicuous head bearing a large compound eye on each side, and a pair of short, thick antennæ. The underside of the abdomen is yellow, but the upper surface is black. The female drills a hole just below the sepals with her saw-like ovipositor, and deposits an egg in the calyx tissue at the base of the stamens. The "sting" mark below the calyx can readily be detected as a minute brown spot, and after practice the egg also can easily be found. After a week or more a small, white, black-headed larva or caterpillar hatches from the egg and enters the side of the fruitlet. It does not enter directly but first tunnels just below the skin. It ultimately reaches and eats out the centre of the young apple. The latter drops from the tree, but not before the larva has deserted it and entered a sound fruit, this time by boring a round hole in the side. Such fruits may be detected by the hole in the side from which a wet mass of black frass and, very often, yellowish fluid exudes. These attacked fruits fall off during June and early July. Occasionally, a newly-hatched larva tunnels beneath the skin of a fruitlet, but for some reason fails to effect an entry. Such a fruit does not fall, but develops normally. The skin, however, splits along the line of the tunnel and a wide, ribbon-like, corky scar is the ultimate result. This is of relatively minor importance, however, for the chief damage is the loss of crop, often very considerable, caused by the dropping of infested fruit.

When fully fed, the larva drops to the ground and spins a tough, brown, parchment-like cocoon an inch or two below the surface of the soil. Here it remains till the spring, when it pupates, finally turning to an adult and emerging from the soil when the apples are in bloom.

Control.—The egg can be killed by an application of nicotine at petal-fall. Care should be taken to drench the trees so that the spray reaches the eye of the fruitlets within a few days of the fall of the petals. If this spray is neglected, all that can be done is to apply a Derris dust when migration and the secondary attack by the young larvæ begin (late in May), in the hope of arresting much of this secondary attack.

CODLING MOTH
(Cydia pomonella)

This insect, like the Apple Sawfly, is responsible for maggoty apples, but its damage may easily be distinguished from that of Sawfly. In the first place, the damage occurs much later—sawfly larvæ having left the trees and most of the damaged fruits having dropped by the end of June, when the first small Codling larvae begin to attack the fruits. Moreover, Codling-damaged apples, if they drop at all, do not do so until shortly before picking time. If an apple is picked for eating and found to be maggoty, it is almost certainly attacked by Codling and not by Sawfly.

By permission of] [Controller, H.M. Stationery Office.

APPLE CAPSID.

1. Foliage attacked by immature Apple Capsid.

2. Attacked fruitlets (early stage).

From the Ministry of Agriculture and Fisheries Advisory Leaflet No. 154.

By courtesy of]   [Dr. H. Wormald.

1. Apple blossom wilt: infected trusses of blossom.

2. A dead spur and canker which has half girdled a branch, taken in winter and showing spore-pustules on spur.

The moth itself does not appear until after petal-fall. It is grey in colour, with dark markings towards the apex of the wings, which have an expanse of about half an inch. It is a very shy creature and is seldom seen, since it flies chiefly at dusk and at sunrise and then only when the air is calm. The eggs are no bigger than a pin's head and are laid on the skin of the fruit or on the leaves. They are inconspicuous and almost transparent.

After hatching, the little white caterpillar eats its way into the fruit either at the eye or through the side, and feeds in the neighbourhood of the core. Often it reveals its presence by the heap of brown excrement which it pushes out of the entrance hole. When fully fed, it leaves the fruit and spins a cocoon in any convenient crevice on the tree. It is usually a pale pink colour by this time and spends the autumn and winter as a larva in the cocoon, turning to a chrysalis in the spring or early summer.

In some seasons, however, a few manage to pupate almost immediately, and a second generation of moths is the result. These give rise to more maggoty apples in September and October.

Control.—Codling is more difficult to contend with than Sawfly. Lead arsenate should be added to the petal-fall spray, which, although applied long before Codling larvæ appear, enables a poisonous deposit to be put into the calyx cup ready for those larvæ which choose to enter the apple at that spot.

Then a further application—and this is the important one—should be made late in June to form the first meal of the larvæ which then begin to go in at the side of the apple. As the egg-laying period is a long one, extending well into July, further applications may have to be made. For all but late-picked varieties these later sprayings should be of Derris and not of lead arsenate. A useful adjunct to spraying is the use of sacking or corrugated paper bands treated with beta-naphthol. After scraping off the loose bark from the tree trunk, the band is affixed before the end of July. Larvæ that enter these bands are killed by the chemical.

RED SPIDER

(Oligonychus ulmi)

This pest has increased since the advent of tar-oil washes which destroy some of the enemies of the Red Spider, but which are ineffective against the pest itself. The small, round, red winter eggs are laid in the autumn on the older twigs. These hatch out when the trees are in bloom, and the young spiders, or "mites," feed on the undersides of the leaves till they are fully grown. Summer, eggs are laid throughout the summer from petal-fall onwards and vast numbers of the mites are sometimes produced, which by their feeding turn the leaves a brownish colour and absorb sap which would normally go into growth or fruit production.

Control.—The lime-sulphur sprays applied for Apple Scab (particularly at petal-fall) are valuable in destroying the active stages of this pest. Sulphur-shy varieties, such as *Lane's Prince Albert*, cannot receive this treatment and for them Derris or a special summer petroleum-oil emulsion is recommended. The most satisfactory control, however, is obtained by the use of a winter petroleum spray in February or March, and this will control Capsid too.

It is necessary to add a word of warning. It sometimes happens that the mites migrate, given suitable weather conditions, and drift through the air. From these migrants late summer attacks can arise, in spite of all previous spray treatment, and require further spraying with lime-sulphur or summer oil.

MINOR PESTS

The foregoing are the most widely occurring and most important insect pests of the apple. There are many others which can be very troublesome at times, such as the Fruit Rhynchites (*Rhynchites æquatus*), which drills holes in the sides of the fruit, the Twig Cutter (*Rhynchites cæruleus*), which cuts off the growing shoots in June, and the Apple Fruit Miner (*Argyresthia conjugella*), which makes holes in the side, and tunnels in the flesh of the fruit.

Mention should also be made of the Clay-coloured Weevil (*Otiorhynchus picipes*), which destroys grafts, and of the Pith

Moth (*Blastodacna hellerella*), the larvæ of which destroy the opening buds.

Other minor pests are the Wood Leopard, the Goat Moth, Clearwing Moth, Lackey Moth, Case-bearers, Shothole Beetles, Scale Insects, and Chafer Beetle Grubs.

DISEASES OF THE APPLE

SCAB *(Venturia inæqualis)*

Often known as Black Spot, this is by far the most prevalent and most destructive disease of apples in this country. It attacks the leaves and fruits of all susceptible varieties and the bud-scales and shoots of some, particularly the shoots of *Cox's Orange Pippin, Lord Suffield* and *Worcester Pearmain*. On these it forms blisterlike pads ("pustules") of fungous tissue that are exposed in spring when the bark covering them splits, and the spores formed on the surface of the pustule are dispersed, probably by wind-blown rain. On the leaves and fruits the disease appears as more or less circular, olive-green spots. These are velvety in texture at first because they are rapidly producing spores, but later they become rather dry and corky in the centre, when they more nearly resemble "scabs." Scab-infection is also responsible for indirect adverse effects. The pustules on the young shoots are a source of entry for the canker fungus, while fruits that are infected early and subsequently crack are victims of fruit-rotting organisms, such as brown rots and moulds, in storage. The crop can be greatly reduced by an early infection of the tiny fruitlets which causes them to drop.

Infection occurs in spring (primary) and throughout the summer months (secondary). As the host-tissues get older they become less susceptible to attack. Infection may arise from spores dispersed from (*a*) dead, over-wintered leaves on the ground, (*b*) pustules on the one-year-old shoots of susceptible varieties, (*c*) pustules on the bud-scales of susceptible varieties, e.g., *Worcester Pearmain*.

The prevalence of the disease greatly depends on the weather conditions in April and May. If, in general, this period is wet and cool, infection is encouraged, for these conditions are very suitable for the growth of the fungus and they tend also to hold the trees for a long period in a very susceptible condition. The converse is equally true. The soil, cultivation, manurial programme and the rootstock can each influence the susceptibility of the host-variety. Excessive nitrogenous manuring, which delays the ripening or "hardening" of the growth, and promotes luxuriant foliage that keeps the tree moist after rain, tends to increase susceptibility to Scab, while potash manuring tends to correct this, although the manurial problem is certainly not as simple as would appear from this generalization.

Control.—There are two chief methods: (*a*) general sanitation which includes collecting and burning, or burying fallen leaves in autumn, and pruning that opens up the head of the tree to light and air, and removes scabbed shoots; (*b*) spraying to protect all new growth as it develops.

Lime-sulphur should be used at the following periods:

(1) *Green-cluster* or *green-bud*, when the short-stalked flower-buds are still tightly clustered, the sepals are mostly covering the petals, and the truss is surrounded by a rosette of half-expanded leaves. Use 2 1/2 per cent.

(2) *Pink-bud*, immediately pre-blossom, when individual flower-buds are well separated, the "cap" of petals not covered by the sepals and showing bold pink, and the truss is surrounded by fully-expanded leaves. Use 2 per cent.

(3) *Petal-fall*. When about three-quarters of the petals have fallen. Use 1 per cent. This spray can cause leaf-burn, leaf-drop, and fruit-drop on certain varieties, which should therefore be omitted from post-blossom applications of lime-sulphur. The chief are *Stirling Castle, Lane's Prince Albert, St. Cecilia*, and *Belle de Boskoop*, none of which are very susceptible under most conditions. It is probably wisest to omit *Stirling Castle* even before blossom, for this variety is excessively sensitive to the proximity of sulphur. In dry, warm summers, *Cox's Orange Pippin, Newton Wonder, Rival, Beauty of Bath, Duchess's Favourite*, and some others, are liable to show leaf- and fruit-drop from this spray. Where previous experience has shown this to be so, the strength may be reduced to 3/4 per cent, or even to 2/3 per cent., or alternatively, a colloidal or other sulphur preparation, used at maker's directions, can be tried, though poor control of Red Spider must then be expected. A mixture of weak lime-sulphur with one of these other sulphur

preparations may also be used.

(4) *Fruitlet*, two weeks after petal-fall. Repeat petal-fall spray.

These four sprayings should suffice, but later ones can be given if necessary. It is always best to spray before infection occurs so that the fungicide can act protectively. Lead arsenate may be mixed with lime-sulphur *before* blossom for the control of caterpillars; indeed, the combined spray is more effective against Scab than lime-sulphur alone. Lead arsenate must not, however, be used with weak lime-sulphur of 1 per cent, or less because of the risk of arsenical spray damage, but there is no such risk in using it with colloidal or similar sulphur preparations. Dusting, either with ground sulphur or with copper-lime dust, is a useful adjunct to spraying, for application can be rapidly made. It should be borne in mind, however, that dust can drift over a wide area, and with sulphur, interplanted sulphur-shy varieties are liable to be adversely affected, while with copper-lime dust, the onset of prolonged, showery weather after application is likely to lead to copper injury on the fruits. This is usually seen as small, purplish-brown, circular, "peppering" of the skin, and its effects can be as severe as those of Scab itself. Copper sprays and dusts are not generally safe on apples, and they are not widely recommended.

The type of soil, the weather conditions, the rootstock, and the manurial treatment each and all influence the trees' susceptibility not only to Scab but also to spray damage. Differing experiences in this connection are thus commonly met with, and no hard and fast ruling is possible.

In general, *Charles Ross, Stirling Castle, Egremont Russet, Belle de Boskoop*, and *King Edward VII* are highly resistant to Scab; *Beauty of Bath, Gladstone, Lord Derby, Early Victoria, Grenadier, Rival, Lane's Prince Albert, John Standish*, and *Duchess's Favourite* are not very susceptible; *Cox's Orange Pippin, Worcester Pearmain, Allington Pippin, Newton Wonder, Bramley's Seedling, Annie Elizabeth, Bismarck, James Grieve, Laxton's Superb*, and *Wellington* are usually very susceptible.

Scab sometimes develops on stored apples, but inadequate spraying early in the season is usually to blame. Spores from older infections are washed over the skin of the fruit in splashing rain just before picking and they give rise to Scab in the store, particularly when the fruit is stored in a moist condition.

CANKER

(Nectria galligena)

This disease is very prevalent in some places, and is commonly said to be associated with poor drainage. At the same time it must be admitted that severe Canker is occasionally found on soils that are well drained though lacking perhaps some other desirable character, and in several instances heavy nitrogenous manuring has been suspect. Infection is most commonly centred around buds or fruit spurs, and not usually in wounds made by pruning until these have healed, when the fungus may become established on the calloused surface. Cankers can also occur where Woolly Aphis or Apple Scab has first attacked the shoots. The cankers often develop elliptically around the centre of infection, making more progress along the length of an affected branch than across the breadth. The cankered area is usually concentrically sunken and discoloured, and fringed, particularly in persistent wet weather, with a ridge of disintegrating stem tissue from which the covering bark flakes irregularly. Sometimes the canker girdles an affected branch, resulting in its death above the canker.

This fungus bears two kinds of fruit-body, each of which occurs on cankered areas: (*a*) Small, whitish pustules burst through the bark, often in rings around the centre of infection. They produce spores plentifully in spring and autumn and following wet periods in summer, and these are capable of causing fresh infections through wounds. (*b*) Crimson, spherical bodies densely clustered together in groups. Superficially, these resemble the eggs of the Fruit Tree Red Spider, but the latter are a brighter red, and are found on healthy as well as on diseased areas. These fruit-bodies produce spores in large quantities in winter and early spring, and are a very real source of danger in the plantation. Apple Canker can also cause an "Eye Rot" of the fruits, but there is a similar disease, "Dry Eye Rot," caused by another fungus, *Botrytis cinerea*, with which it can easily be confused.

Control.—The best method is to cut out the cankers as soon as they are seen, and before the fruit-bodies have been produced. A sharp gouge, or hollow-ground chisel, is very useful for this work with older cankers where the wood is affected. All diseased tissue, and dead or dying branches, should be removed and burnt. Though it is commonly held that the wounds should be dressed with a white-lead paint to prevent reinfection, experience shows that if the cankers are thoroughly cleaned out painting is unnecessary, except on varieties prone to Silver Leaf infection (see page 170). The normal programme of sprays for Scab control has little direct effect on the incidence of Canker, but the control of Scab and Woolly Aphis is indirectly helpful. Badly-drained soil should be aerated by some system of drainage.

Many commercial and garden varieties are susceptible, notably: *Worcester Pearmain, James Grieve, Laxton's Superb, Ellison's Orange, Warner's King, Beauty of Bath*, and *Cox's Orange Pippin*. This last is more susceptible on No. XII and No. XVI than on most other stocks in the Malling series. *Bramley's Seedling, Grenadier, Early Victoria, Gladstone*, and *Newton Wonder* are among the most resistant.

BROWN ROTS.

(See also Plum, page 314.)

Blossom Wilt and Spur Canker (Sclerotinia laxa, forma mali).

The flowers become infected by spores from pustules on dead twigs and withered flowers infected during the previous year. Sometimes the whole flower-truss withers and dies when the fungus grows down the flower-stalks and into the spur, forming a canker there which sometimes extends into the branch and kills it. The variety *Lord Derby* is very susceptible, trees being sometimes so badly infected that the branch system is almost completely destroyed by the disease.

Control.—Cankered branches and spurs should be promptly cut out and burnt, for *grey-coloured* pustules of spores arise on them in the following spring, and these can, in their turn, infect the flower-trusses and so continue the disease-cycle. Spraying late in the dormant period with 5 per cent, tar-distillate wash, very thoroughly applied, burns up the fungus pustules on any dead spurs that may have been overlooked in the cutting out. It is thought that this fungus is distinct from that which causes Blossom Wilt of plums and cherries, hence, that apples are not likely to be infected from plums and cherries.

Brown Rot (Sclerotinia fructigena).

This disease causes heavy loss of picked fruits every year, The fungus produces a brown, soft rot of the fruits on the tree, usually within a few weeks of picking-time, and also after they are picked and stored. Spore-pustules are very readily produced on an infected fruit (often in concentric rings around the point of infection). Under certain storage conditions, however, a fruit may turn black, and may bear few or no pustules.

The fungus gains entry through a blemish where the skin has been pierced; this may happen in many ways—bird pecks, insect punctures, cracking following Scab or spray-injury, hail or spur damage, rough handling during picking operations, etc. A diseased fruit is capable of infecting a healthy one by persistent contact on the tree or in the orchard box. It is wise, therefore, to discard blemished apples at picking-time and during the preliminary sorting before the fruits are graded.

A *spur-canker* similar to that caused by the Blossom-Wilt fungus sometimes occurs on soft-wooded varieties such as *Lord Derby* or *James Grieve*. This arises when the fungus grows along the fruit-stalk and into the spur.

Control.—Dead spurs, which early in the following summer bear relatively large, *buff-coloured* pustules of spores (by which this fungus can be distinguished from that causing Blossom Wilt and Spur Canker) should be cut out and burnt. If infected fruits are permitted to remain on the tree, they become mummified, and, in late spring and summer, are covered with the familiar buff-coloured spore-pustules. Mummied fruits should be removed and burnt where they persist for they are a common source of infection. The spores are light and powdery when dry, and are easily blown about in the wind. They are also carried by insects.

SOOTY BLOTCH
(Glœodes pomigena)
(See Plum, page 316.)

APPLE MILDEW
(Podosphæra leucotricha)

Affected shoots and leaves are white and mealy; flower-trusses present a similar appearance, and the flowers are small and distorted and often fail to open. The buds become infected in summer and remain all winter with the fungus spawn alive between the bud-scales. Such buds grow out into mildewed shoots in spring or they may be killed and fail to start into growth. The powdery spores produced on affected shoots and leaves carry infection to healthy tissues throughout the summer; the spores are mainly wind-borne. A winter stage in the form of tiny, black fruit-bodies, produced mainly on the shoots, is thought to have little influence in this country in the annual cycle of the fungus.

Occasionally the fruits are affected. *Lane's Prince Albert* is a susceptible variety to this form of attack. Affected fruits bear the whitish, mealy fungus-tissue on the surface of the skin.

Control.—Cut out and burn infected shoots and flower-trusses, and spray as for Apple Scab.

Among susceptible varieties are *Lane's Prince Albert, Cox's Orange Pippin, Bismarck, Bramley's Seedling, Allington Pippin. Worcester Pearmain* is resistant.

ARMILLARIA ROOT ROT

(Honey Fungus—*Armillaria mellea*)

This fungus is commonly found in woodlands, and it frequently causes a serious disease of conifers and of broad-leaved trees. It spreads underground by means of strands of fungous tissue that look rather like black boot-laces; indeed, the disease is often said to be caused by the "Boot-lace Fungus." When these "bootlaces" come into contact with the roots of fruit trees, they are able to attack them, causing infection which spreads back along the infected roots to the collar of the tree. Eventually all the feeding roots may be affected and the tree dies. This may happen suddenly if the collar of the tree is soon girdled by the fungal strands. The fungus produces sporing fructifications, usually in autumn, on the dead stump and on the surface of the soil immediately surrounding it. These fructifications are like toadstools and are usually densely clustered together. The "umbrella" of each "toadstool" may be from 2 to 4 inches across; it is honey-coloured and, when young, often bears dark scales on its upper surface. The bark of a dead tree can readily be peeled off, and underneath, between it and the wood, fan-like layers of white fungous tissue, sometimes flecked with black lines, will be found. These layers have a distinct fungous odour.

The fungus attacks not only apples but pears, plums, cherries, gooseberries, and even strawberries. The leaves usually show the first symptoms; they are yellow, sickly, and may be wilting, often over the whole tree, but since there are other possible causes (see Waterlogging on next page) an accurate diagnosis must depend on the presence or absence of the fungus.

Control.—It is most important that trees dying from attack by Armillaria Root Rot should be promptly removed and burnt. The digging-out of broken roots must be thorough and the sites of affected trees should be kept cultivated and, if planted up at all, used for annual crops such as potatoes for several years before being replanted with fruit. Frequent stirring of the soil breaks up any "boot-laces" or bits of affected root that remain, helps to dry them out and prevents the fungus from becoming re-established on the roots of weeds, which help to keep it going. Close watch must be kept on adjoining trees for the first symptoms of attack, and any that show these should also be promptly removed and destroyed, for only in this way can an outbreak be checked. Cleared woodland is best put down to arable crops for at least three or four years before fruit is planted up, otherwise there is considerable risk of infection.

Since the fungus can also attack fencing poles, these should be well creosoted before setting up.

When thinning out overcrowded plantations, it is bad practice to leave tree-stumps in the ground, for the fungus can become established on them by means of spores dispersed from the toadstools.

CROWN GALL

(Bacterium tumefaciens)

This bacterium occurs in the soil and infects the roots of apple stocks and many other plants including raspberries, loganberries, and blackberries. Wounds are a common source of entry. The bacterium produces galls or tumours of up to several inches in diameter on the roots and on the stems near soil level. East Malling No. VII rootstock is particularly susceptible and the scion variety is said to influence the susceptibility of the stock.

The galls probably have little adverse effect on the tree in most cases.

Control.—Affected stocks should not be planted in nurseries and precautions should be taken to protect wounded surfaces from infection; e.g., by covering with grafting-wax, or by dipping the roots in a mercurial preparation.

SILVER LEAF

This disease is described under Plum, page 315. In apple the most susceptible variety is *Newton Wonder*, infection often being associated with a condition popularly known as "Papery Bark." The danger to *Newton* is in *top*-grafting it to another variety, when large wounds must be made on established trees. These wounds provide a ready place of entry for the fungus, and they are therefore best avoided by using one of the modern methods of framework grafting (see page 49).

FUNCTIONAL DISEASES

These are non-parasitic diseases due to some disorder in the life-processes of the plant. They are not caused by a fungus or by any other organism of that nature.

WATERLOGGING

The leaf symptoms are similar in some respects to those caused by Armillaria Root Rot in that the foliage wilts and looks sickly. Where Waterlogging, also popularly known as "The Death," is the cause, the wilting usually occurs fairly suddenly and within a few weeks after growth starts in the spring, and it may affect only certain branches or parts of them. An affected tree may have looked quite healthy during the previous year, whereas with Armillaria Root Rot the chronic stage is frequently preceded by symptoms of steady decline. The signs of fungus attack present with Armillaria—toadstools in autumn, "boot-laces" in the soil, a mat of fungus under the bark near the soil—are absent with Waterlogging, and the clue to the cause of the trouble will be found in the root-system. Some of the larger roots show internal, and possibly external, discoloration, and they often have an alcoholic smell when freshly cut. This is due to their having been asphyxiated in a soil where the air has been excluded by excessive moisture, especially in badly-drained soils or pockets of soil during very wet weather in autumn and winter. In severe cases the affected tree dies, though in mild cases only certain branches, or even flower-trusses here and there, may wilt and die. Another form of the disease is sometimes found when inefficiently staked trees that have been rocked by autumn gales and have then been subjected to heavy rains show a rotting and discoloration of the bark of the collar at ground level, even in an apparently well-drained soil. Here, the soil surrounding the collar has been "puddled" by the intermittent pressure of the swaying trunk and by frequent rain, it becomes impervious, and the excess water collects in the crater so formed, eventually resulting in rotting at the collar and the death of the tree.

Symptoms superficially similar to those of a mild attack of Water-logging are caused by excessive spraying with tar- or petroleum-oil, but in this case, though the bark may be blackened, the roots usually show no sign of disease, and the buds either fail to break, or fail to develop leaves after starting into growth. Severe potash-deficiency occasionally results in the wilting and death in spring of flower-trusses on individual branches of trees, though here, as in Armillaria Root Rot, the appearance of sickliness is a gradual, and not a sudden, process. It can be identified in earlier stages by general debility and a scorching of the margins of the leaves in summer. (See Leaf-Scorch, below.)

Control.—Some system of drainage must be adopted for

inefficiently drained and very retentive soils. Shallower planting on such soils also is recommended. Very badly drained soils should not be planted with fruit. Efficient staking of trees, especially where they are exposed to gales, will do much to prevent the "collar-rot" form. As no organism is responsible for this disease, an affected tree is not a source of infection for its neighbours. Some form of this disorder has been found on almost every type of fruit grown in this country (e.g., see Root Rot in Strawberries).

LEAF-SCORCH

The symptoms are best seen in summer when the leaves (especially the older ones) of an affected tree have a reddish-brown margin, sometimes, in bad cases, 1/2 inch deep. Towards the end of summer, these margins become dark-brown, dry and crisp, and the leaves are "hard" and usually up-curled. The fruits on such a tree are often smaller than normal, lack colour and flavour, and do not store well. Trees on certain rootstocks, e.g., East Mailing No. II and No. V, are particularly susceptible, and *Cox's Orange Pippin* and *Bramley's Seedling* are susceptible varieties.

Control.—This form of Leaf-Scorch can be controlled by regular applications of a potassic manure (e.g., sulphate of potash at 3-4 cwt. per acre) to restore the nutritional balance.

The symptoms should not be confused with those of lime-sulphur injury, which are superficially similar but are seen usually within a week of a spray-application. Furthermore, the *young* leaves, as well as the older ones, are affected, the spray-burn being present in reddish patches, often, but not always, concentrated around the leaf-margins, which later turn dark brown and die.

A different form of Leaf-Scorch from that caused by shortage of available potash is sometimes found on apples, and it is due to a shortage of available magnesium in the soil. The chief symptom is a thin "feel" with discoloration between the veins, and later in the season these areas die and become brown, thus giving rise to the usual descriptive phrase "interveinal scorch," as opposed to the "marginal scorch" of potash deficiency. The fruits are poor and lack flavour in severe cases. Magnesium deficiency is most usually found on light soils deficient in lime, and is most pronounced in wet seasons. An interesting practical point is that symptoms of magnesium deficiency can be induced on some soils by the too liberal use of artificial potassic manure to correct potash deficiency.

Control.—Magnesian limestone should be substituted for ordinary lime in the normal process of liming acid soils. A top-dressing of dung to established trees would also be helpful. These deficiencies are not confined to apples among the fruits; pears, gooseberries, currants, strawberries, raspberries, plums, and cherries are all liable to be affected.

CHLOROSIS

This disease can affect pears, plums, cherries, and soft fruits as well as apples, the typical symptoms being pronounced loss of green colour and consequent yellowing or even bleaching of the leaves, especially those on the young growths. It is caused by deficiency of available iron, which, though necessary for healthy plant growth in only very small quantities—it is a so-called "trace element"—is nevertheless essential to the proper functioning of the leaves. Without iron the leaves are unable to form the green colouring matter (chlorophyll) on which the nutrition of the plant depends.

Chlorosis is commonly associated with fruit trees growing in soils rich in lime, and is thus frequently referred to as "lime-induced" Chlorosis.*

Control.—Since Chlorosis is due more usually to lack of availability of iron than to its absence, the disease is not likely to be curable by the application of iron salts to the soil, especially where the Chlorosis is "lime-induced." Spraying the leaves with ferrous sulphate at 4 lb. per 100 gallons as a constituent of the 1 per cent. post-blossom lime-sulphur spray for Scab is effective, or solid compounds of iron, such as ferric citrate or tartrate, can be injected into holes bored in the trunk or branches. Grassing-down, too, tends to cure Chlorosis.

BITTER PIT

Within a few weeks before picking-time, affected fruits show scattered, slightly sunken, circular areas, in the skin, often on only one side of the fruit. The spots vary in colour from dark green to brownish-green. If the skin covering an affected area of fruit be peeled off, the flesh immediately underneath each sunken area will be seen to be collapsed and brown in little pockets of up to a quarter of an inch in diameter. The pockets are not usually very deep-seated in the flesh, but are more often near, or at the surface. This disease is known as "tree pit." "Storage pit," another form with the same, or similar, underlying causes, occurs in apples after a period of storage, though the fruits may have seemed quite normal when picked. In storage pit, especially in the early stages, the skin is often not sunken but merely mottled, though when the flesh of the fruit is exposed, numerous, scattered pockets, pinkish-brown in colour, will be seen sometimes extending nearly to the core. These pockets tend to be smaller individually than those of tree-pit, and are often concentrated at the calyx end.

The cause of these troubles is very complex and rather obscure. Hard pruning; hot, dry weather (particularly when accompanied by hot winds); and, with storage pit, too-early picking, are all said to predispose the fruit to the disorder. Bitter Pit is often met with on fruit from young trees just coming into bearing and on those from older trees with only a light crop. Heavy nitrogenous manuring also is suspect.

Control.—The grower is able to control some of these factors, and his general line of attack is to do all he can to promote steady, balanced growth throughout the season, to check biennial bearing as much as possible by judicious pruning and crop regulation, and to avoid any practice likely to cause violent fluctuations in the reaction of the trees. To some extent, however, he must be at the mercy of the weather. Bitter Pit has been observed in many varieties. Most of the better-known ones are liable to show symptoms under appropriate conditions, but among these, *Allington Pippin, Newton Wonder, Edward VII, Bramley's Seedling, Lane's Prince Albert*, and *Cox's Orange Pippin* are perhaps the worst offenders.

"GLASSINESS" OR WATER-CORE

Affected apples show yellowish areas, which appear to be water-soaked or "glassy," in the flesh and often around the core. Natural recovery sometimes occurs, but apples prone to Glassiness are liable eventually to develop Bitter Pit. In severe cases, affected fruits appear to have been badly bruised, and in advanced cases, an extensive, discoloured "crinkle" may appear on the surface.

The underlying causes are rather obscure but are known to be similar to those of tree pit. (See page 173.) The varieties *Rival, St. Everard*, and *Lord Lambourne* are prone to Glassiness.

LENTICEL SPOT

Certain varieties, *Allington Pippin* prominent among them, are specially prone to develop small, brown, often sunken spots centred around the lenticels or breathing pores of the fruit. Again, the main cause is functional, though soft fungal rots may eventually set in at some of the affected places. The trouble is much worse in some seasons than others and affected fruits store badly. Soil and weather conditions are thought to be largely responsible. Fruits that develop Lenticel Spot also frequently show symptoms of other functional disorders.

Control.—As with Bitter Pit and Glassiness, the grower can do little apart from striving to maintain steady growth conditions.

SUN SCALD

Following a period of very high temperature in summer, apples and other fruits may show signs of burning on the exposed sunny side. Such conditions occurred at the end of August, 1942, when Sun Scald was very prevalent on apples. Severely affected fruits showed circular, brown, flattened areas sometimes surrounded by a bright, reddish halo, while those only slightly affected showed roughly circular, pale areas or deeper flushes of colour, depending on the variety. Occasionally, and especially on *Allington*, the affected area resembled a bruise, and was arc-like and sunken, and of a deep red or purplish-red colour. The baked, brown area on severely affected fruits was commonly a source of entry for the Brown Rot fungus.

Control.—There is no means of control under commercial conditions where shading would clearly be impracticable, but in gardens it might be feasible to shade the fruits by some simple means in the hottest part of the day during heat-wave conditions. The malady is not of frequent occurrence in this country.

DISEASES AND PESTS: DIAGNOSIS TABLE

DAMAGE	PROBABLE CAUSE
BRANCHES AND TWIGS	**PESTS**
Patches of "woolly" white substance; gall-like swellings	American Blight (Woolly Aphis)
Branches tunnelled	Goat Moth or Wood Leopard Moth
	DISEASES
Cankerous formations—patches of small, whitish pustules or crimson spherical bodies grouped together	Canker

Sheets of fungous tissue under bark at base of trunk. Long black strands like "boot-laces" on roots and in adjacent soil; tree dies	Armillaria
Galls on roots	Crown Gall

SHOOTS AND FOLIAGE (INCLUDING BLOSSOM)	**PESTS**
Leaves, opening buds and blossom attacked by small "looping," green caterpillars	Winter Moths
Leaves and buds eaten and spun together by small brown, green or yellowish caterpillars which wriggle quickly backwards when disturbed. Eaten buds wilt or shrivel and turn brown. Leaves again attacked in mid-July	Tortrix Moths

Leaves curled and attacked by masses of small, green or bluish-purple aphides. Young shoots twisted, stunted and deformed	Greenfly or Rosy Apple Aphis
Flower buds eaten from within in April by black-headed white grub; blossoms remain capped, turn brown, and drop	Apple Blossom Weevil
Buds attacked by yellow to pale green, flattish, aphis-like creature; buds turn brown and drop after opening. Drops of white, sticky wax proclaim nature of trouble	Apple Sucker
Small black marks turning brown and then into holes on young leaves—quickly moving aphis-like creatures. Young shoots distorted and with corky scars	Capsid Bug
Leaves turn brownish	Red Spider

Growing shoots cut off in June	Twig Cutter

DISEASES

Leaves and shoots white and mealy; flowers small and distorted, may fail to open, trusses white and mealy	Apple Mildew
Blister-like "pustules" on shoots and possibly on bud scales in Spring. Circular, olive-green spots, turning corky and scab-like later	Scab
Silvery sheen foliage on affected branch—brown stain in wood	"Silver Leaf"
Flowers wither, turn brown and die; subsequently spurs cankered with grey pustules	Brown Rot, Blossom Wilt

Apparently healthy tree wilts or fails to grow soon after bud burst; blossom trusses and surrounding leaves only may be affected above ground	Waterlogging
Reddish-brown margins to leaves in summer, becoming dark-brown, "hard" and usually up-curled	Potash-deficiency. Leaf Scorch
Brownish, scorched areas between veins, leaves feel thin.	Magnesium - deficiency. Leaf Scorch
Leaves yellow or bleached particularly on young growths	Chlorosis

FRUIT	**PESTS**
Small fruits eaten by green, "looping" caterpillars	Winter Moths
Small patches of skin on developed fruit eaten by tiny larvæ	Tortrix Moths

Small deformed and disfigured fruits, corky scars	Apple Capsid Bug
Fruits drop off in June and July—hole in side with wet mass of black frass exuding; long, corky lines on fruits may be present	Apple Sawfly
Maggoty apples; may drop just before picking-time	Codling Moth
Holes drilled in sides of fruits	Fruit Rhynchites
Holes drilled in sides of fruits and tunnels in flesh	Apple Fruit Miner
Brown, often sunken areas around lenticels	Lenticel Spot
Spherical discoloured areas on sunny side of fruit, may be pale, flushed, or brown	Sun Scald

DISEASES

Eye-rot of ripening fruit	Canker

Brown, soft rot of fruit on tree (usually within few weeks of picking), also while stored; buff spore pustules often in rings. Stored fruit may turn black; fruit left on tree becomes mummified	Brown Rot
Brownish, roughly circular, indefinite smudges on skin (usually near picking-time)	Sooty Blotch
Skin white and mealy	Apple Mildew
Circular olive-green spots, velvety at first, turning corky and scab-like in summer	Scab
Slightly sunken, small, dark green to brownish-green spots within a few weeks before picking; brownish pockets in flesh after picking	Bitter Pit

Once the trouble has been diagnosed, the reader should refer to the paragraph dealing with the particular disease and pest, and also to the Guide to Spraying, see page 142.

VARIETIES OF APPLE

With all the knowledge that is now available on the subject of apple culture, it should be possible to grow any variety successfully provided its particular requirements in such matters as manuring and cross-pollination are known. By force of circumstance, however, most of this experimental data has been obtained from a comparatively small number of commercial varieties, and such information as is available about the so-called garden varieties is of an empirical nature, based on the observations of a large number of individuals working under varying conditions. This accounts for the wide differences of opinion so frequently expressed at horticultural club meetings and at shows concerning merits and demerits of any particular "garden" variety. It is a pity that the great work which is being done for commercial varieties of fruits by the Royal Horticultural Society in the National Fruit Trials at Wisley, cannot be repeated for garden varieties grown under garden conditions. Many varieties, both new and old, which would never survive the rigorous tests to which a commercial variety is submitted, might well assume a new importance when grown under the more congenial conditions of a garden; other varieties which still figure in nurserymen's catalogues might, under official trial, be definitely relegated to the obscurity for which they have been long overdue, whilst yet a third class, once condemned for some fault of growth, cropping or disease, might yet yield to treatment under modern methods and so regain their lost popularity.

WINTER PRUNING.

Bush Apple "Lane's Prince Albert" (six years old).

Before and after Pruning.

Copyright Photo.   (East Malling Research Station.

* For further particulars, see Ministry of Agriculture and Fisheries Bulletin No. 49.

* Laterals which are so strong as to be positively gross are called by the French "gourmands"; these are best cut clean put at the base.

* Chlorosis can in some stages be confused with nitrogen or other deficiency symptoms. (See "The Diagnosis of Mineral Deficiencies in Plants" by Dr. T. Wallace.)

DESCRIPTIVE NOTES ON VARIETIES

DESSERT APPLES

Adam's Pearmain. A medium-sized conical apple, red and yellow with russet. Fine flavour. Season, December to March. Upright habit. Makes thin branches. An excellent late apple for the garden.

Advance. See Laxton's Advance.

Allington Pippin. A round, medium-sized apple, primrose-yellow with red. Season, October to January. A curious flavour not liked by all. Good cropper. Good when baked. Tree makes very twiggy growth and needs skilful pruning. Best grown as espalier. Susceptible to capsid bug. Liable to Lenticel spot in store.

American Mother. A medium-sized, conical-shaped fruit, rich yellow, flushed and striped deep red. Yellow flesh. Sweet and aromatic. Season, October. Uncertain cropper. Makes a good garden standard.

Barnack Beauty. A medium-sized conical apple, yellow and red with handsome open eye. Season, December to March. Crisp and acid flavour. A tip-bearer best grown as a bush. Somewhat shy cropper. Said to succeed on chalky subsoils.

Beauty of Bath. A small, round, flat apple, brilliant dappled scarlet, widely grown for market as a first early. Season, early August. Strong growth, untidy habit and rather tip-bearing. Slow bearer. Very difficult to train in any artificial form. Fruit drops easily. Flavour fair and crisp but not first-rate.

Belle de Boskoop. Medium to large round apple, rather like a Blenheim Orange. Season, December to April. Very strong grower, useful for top-grafting on to standard trees. A very good flavour when ripe, but unattractive in appearance. Triploid variety, see page 191, and needs cross-pollinator diploid variety. (See colour plate facing page 193.)

Blenheim Orange. A medium to large-sized, flattish, round apple, rich golden-yellow, tinged and striped red and russeted. Fine flavour, firm yellow flesh. Season, November to January. Dessert or cooking. Good cropper when established but usually takes some years to come into full bearing. Stores well. Does well on medium loam and heavy soils, and in grass orchards. Forms strong and spreading standard or bush and needs maximum space. Does well as bush on East Mailing No. IX. Prune hard to form tree and then lightly. Susceptible to scab and canker. Triploid variety, see page 191, and needs cross-pollinator diploid variety.

Brownlees Russet. A medium-sized, flattish and irregular-shaped apple, a reddish-brown and green russet. Excellent flavour, tender, greenish-white flesh, sharp but sweet and juicy. Season, January to April. A good cropper and stores well. A fine garden fruit, usually grown in bush form. Self-sterile.

Calville Blanche. A round medium-sized dessert apple, pale yellow. Season, January to April. Widely grown in France. Does well under glass.

Charles Ross. A large-sized, beautiful round apple, very similar in appearance to Peasgood Nonsuch, highly coloured, a greenish-yellow, streaked with red and patched with russet. Fair flavour, brisk, sweet and juicy. Season, September to November. A good cropper but does not store well and should therefore be used as soon as possible after picking. Thrives in chalky soils and in any locality. Best grown as pyramid or bush. The fruit is too large for cordon culture. Recommended for pot culture. A fine exhibition fruit and popular market variety, but not recommended for orchard culture. Self-sterile. Resistant to scab but susceptible to canker and capsid bug.

Christmas Pearmain. A medium-sized, round to conical apple, rosy cheek and russeted. Fine flavour, crisp flesh, slightly sub-acid. Season, December to January. Good bearer. Upright and neat in growth and recommended for inclusion in small private gardens in bush or cordon form. Said to be partially self-fertile.

Claygate Pearmain. A medium-sized, round to conical apple, somewhat similar to Ribston Pippin, dull green, flushed reddish-brown and russeted. Fine flavour, tender greenish-white flesh, luscious and aromatic. Season, December to February. A good cropper and stores well if gathered when perfectly ripe. Makes a big, spreading tree in standard form, but some growers recommend bush-form culture only. Recommended for garden culture. One of the best late dessert apples. Self-sterile.

Cornish Gillyflower. A medium-sized, oval and conical apple, ribbed at top, yellowish-green and red and thinly russeted. Excellent flavour, crisp yellowish-white flesh. Season, December to February. Of somewhat straggly growth. A good cropper in mild districts. Tip-bearer. Self-sterile.

Cox's Orange Pippin. A medium-sized, round to conical apple, a golden to orange and red russet skin. Delicious flavour, tender yellowish-white flesh, luscious and aromatic. A good cropper, storing well. Season, November to January. Does well only in well-, but not excessively-drained soils. In the colder districts the shelter of a wall should be provided. Medium vigour but twiggy in growth. It makes a fair orchard tree on loamy soil. Also grown as bush, espalier and cordon. Recommended for private garden culture. Also suitable for pot culture. Needs regular pruning and heavy potash supplies. Self-sterile, but cross-pollinates well with Worcester Pearmain and James Grieve. (See colour plate facing page 193.)

Crimson Cox's Orange Pippin. This is merely a coloured bud-sport of the above—a deep claret-coloured apple otherwise possessing all the characteristics of Cox's Orange Pippin.

D'Arcy Spice. A medium-sized, roundish, flattened and ribbed apple, a brownish russet over dull yellow. Excellent flavour, firm greenish flesh, sweet, juicy and aromatic. Season,

March to May. A fair cropper but needs very careful handling and storing. Comes from Essex, where it is much prized but considered difficult to grow. Self-sterile.

Devonshire Quarrenden. A small, roundish, flattened apple, a deep crimson in Colour. Good flavour, crisp greenish flesh, juicy and refreshing. Season, August to September. A good cropper but does not keep in store. Does well almost anywhere and in any kind of soil. Forms an upright standard, pyramid, bush or cordon. An old English favourite early dessert apple. *Extremely susceptible to scab.* Self-sterile. Fruit too small for modern markets.

Duchess's Favourite. A small, attractive-looking apple of distinctive appearance, bright "cricket-ball" crimson, with a markedly open eye. Once widely grown for market, but now considered too small. Season, September. Distinctly woody texture. Needs fruit thinning. Small tree.

Duke of Devonshire. A small to medium-sized, round apple, a dull yellow, tinged with russet. Excellent flavour, crisp flesh, juicy, sweet and aromatic. Season, March to April. A good cropper and storing well. Gather in October. Makes a good standard or may be grown as espalier, bush or cordon. Suitable for garden culture. One of the best of the late dessert apples. *Highly resistant to scab.* Said to be partially self-fertile.

Egremont Russet. A medium-sized, round and flattish apple, golden yellow and russeted. Very good flavour, firm greenish flesh, crisp and sweet. Season, October to November.

A good cropper for immediate use. A good garden variety, forming a neat standard, pyramid or bush. One of the most attractive and best of the russets. Said to be partially self-fertile. Resistant to scab.

Ellison's Orange. A fairly large-sized, round to conical apple, said to be a cross between Cox and Calville Blanche, somewhat similar to Cox's Orange Pippin in shape and colour. Greenish-yellow, streaked with red. Of tender yellowish flesh, luscious and aromatic. Flavour not universally popular. Season, September to October. A good cropper for immediate use. Does well on almost any soil, thriving in the Midlands and Northern Counties. Forms an upright, neat standard or bush and is recommended for garden culture. Also grown as cordon. A popular market fruit. Said to be partially self-fertile. Good for top grafting.

Exquisite. See Laxton's Exquisite.

Fortune. See Laxton's Fortune.

Gladstone. See Mr. Gladstone.

Golden Reinette. See Heusgen's Golden Reinette.

Heusgen's Golden Reinette. A medium-sized, round and flattened apple, bright scarlet and russeted over. Good flavour, crisp yellowish flesh. Season, March. A good cropper and keeps well. Grown as standard, bush or espalier. Makes a small tree. Recommended for garden culture. One of the best of the late dessert apples. Self-sterile.

Irish Peach. A small-sized, roundish to conical and

flattened apple, pale yellow, mottled and streaked red. Good flavour, tender greenish flesh, rich and aromatic. This is about the earliest of all dessert apples. Season, July to August. A fairly good cropper but does not keep and is best eaten as gathered. Does well in the Midlands and Northern districts. Apt to make a weak standard and is best grown in bush form. Prune lightly. A fine early dessert apple. Said to be partially self-fertile. *Very early flowerer.*

James Grieve. A medium-sized, round to conical apple, greenish-yellow, striped and tinged with red. Fine flavour, soft yellowish flesh, juicy and sweet. Season, September to October. Good cropper but does not keep in store. For market it should be picked in August and September while still hard and green, and to obtain large fruit, heavy thinning is necessary. Makes a compact neat bush excellent for private gardens or for growing in pots. Does well in the Midlands and the colder Northern counties. Susceptible to canker and brown rot. Said to be partly self-fertile.

John Standish. A small-sized, roundish and flattened apple, bright red in colour. Good flavour, firm white flesh, luscious and sweet. Season, December to March or April. A good cropper and keeping well. Grown as standard, bush, espalier or cordon. A useful late dessert. Self-sterile. Not of first-class flavour.

King of the Pippins. A medium-sized, roundish, oblong-shaped apple, a deep golden-yellow flushed reddish-brown.

Fair flavour, crisp yellowish-white flesh, juicy and slightly sharp. Season, October to December. A prolific cropper and keeping well. Does best in the warmer districts and in light, well-drained soil. Makes a medium-sized, upright standard, bush, espalier or cordon. Said to be partially self-fertile.

King's Acre Pippin. A medium-sized, round to conical apple, somewhat similar in appearance to Ribston Pippin, dull yellowish-orange, warmly flushed and russeted. Excellent flavour, firm, yellowish flesh, juicy and highly flavoured. Season, January to March. A medium cropper and stores well. Forms a moderately robust standard, bush or trained tree. Suitable for garden culture. Needs a warm sunny situation to colour well. A good late dessert apple. Said to be partially self-fertile.

Lady Sudeley. A fairly large-sized round to conical and flat-shaped apple, a rich golden-yellow, with crimson stripes. Good flavour, tender, yellowish flesh, juicy and crisp. Season, August to September. A prolific cropper but will not keep and is best eaten as soon as possible after picking. Does well in all soils and situations, including colder localities, in standard, bush, espalier or cordon form. Recommended for garden and pot culture. Said to be partially self-fertile.

Langley Pippin. A small-sized, tall, conical-shaped apple, yellow with crimson blotches and streaks. Good flavour, soft, yellowish flesh, juicy and pleasant. Season, August to September. A good cropper but does not keep and is best eaten as soon after picking as possible. Likes a medium loam soil and forms a moderately weak, drooping tree. May be grown as espalier. Not an orchard fruit. Self-sterile.

Laxton's Advance. A small to medium-sized, round to conical apple, a bright crimson in colour. A cross between Cox's Orange Pippin and Mr. Gladstone, recently introduced. Good flavour, with crisp and juicy flesh. Season, early August. Does not keep and is best eaten as soon as possible after picking. Recommended for garden culture. Self-sterile.

Laxton's Epicure. A medium-sized, flattened, round apple, a pale yellow, flushed and striped bright crimson. Good flavour, tender, yellowish flesh, juicy and sweet. Season, September. Best eaten as soon after picking as possible. Grown in all forms. Suitable for garden culture. Said to be self-fertile.

Laxton's Exquisite. A fairly large-sized, round to oval apple, yellow flaked and streaked red. Fine flavour, tender and juicy, similar to Cox's Orange Pippin. Season, September to October. A good cropper for immediate use. The fruit should be picked as soon as ready and not left too long on the tree. A very good second-early dessert apple. Said to be self-fertile. Susceptible to scab.

Laxton's Fortune. Medium round to conical apple, rosy red when ripe. Very juicy and sweet. Season, October to November. One of the most promising of new varieties. Tree of medium vigour. Suitable for garden culture. Flowers with Cox.

Laxton's Pearmain. A medium to large, round to conical and flattened apple, yellowish, tinted ruddy brown and rosy cheek. Fine flavour, firm, yellowish flesh, sweet and juicy. Season, December to April. Keeps well. Recommended for private garden culture. Said to be self-fertile.

Laxton's Superb. A large to medium-sized, round to conical and flattened apple, green to yellow flushed red and rosy cheek. Fine flavour, crisp, white flesh, juicy, sweet and aromatic. Season, November to March. A good cropper and keeps well. Makes a strong and spreading standard or bush. Also grown as espalier or cordon. Recommended for private garden culture. Has been widely planted in recent years.

Lord Lambourne. A medium-sized, round to conical apple, a rich red flushed over yellow. Good flavour, firm, yellowish flesh, juicy and sweet but greasy. Season, October to December. A good cropper but does not keep long. Makes a fine strong standard or bush, espalier or cordon. Recommended for private garden culture.

May Queen. Medium size, yellow and red with some russet. Good flavour. Very late. Season, November to May. Makes small tree. Suitable for small garden.

Melba. A large round dessert apple, pinkish red with marked bloom, very juicy. Season, end of August. A Canadian variety.

Mr. Gladstone. A medium-sized, round to conical and ribbed apple, yellow flushed and striped dark red. Fair flavour, soft, greenish flesh, juicy and aromatic. Season, July to August. A good cropper for immediate use, preferably eaten as picked. Does well in the Midlands and in Northern localities. Somewhat weak grower and a tip-bearer. Best grown as a bush. One of the earliest dessert apples. Unsuitable for artificial forms of culture. Does not respond well to spur pruning. Said to be partially self-fertile.

Miller's Seedling. A small to medium-sized oval apple, yellow with primrose flush. Season, August to September only. One of the juiciest apples. Much in demand on the London market in some seasons. A weak grower but neat and upright in habit. *Fruit must be thinned.* Suitable for small bush, fuseau or cordon. Recommended for garden culture. Quite unsuitable for standard.

Ontario. See list of Cooking Apples.

Orleans Reinette. A medium-sized, flattened round-shaped apple, somewhat similar to a Blenheim Orange but smaller. A golden russet, flushed deep red. Superb flavour, sweet, crisp and juicy. Some experts maintain this to be the best flavoured of all dessert apples. Season, December to February. A fair cropper and storing well. Makes a strong-growing standard or bush, espalier or cordon. One of the best dessert apples. Said to be partially self-fertile. Somewhat susceptible to canker. Apt to shrivel in store if picked too soon.

Owen Thomas. A small early dessert apple, a cross between Cox's Orange Pippin and Mr. Gladstone. Makes a weak, straggling tree. Good for gardens but unsuitable for orchard culture. The fruit resembles that of Mr. Gladstone, but has a distinct Cox's Orange flavour. Season, August.

Patricia. A large round dessert apple, cricket ball red, very juicy. Season, early September. A Canadian variety.

Pitmaston Pine Apple. Small conical golden russet with yellow flesh. Of exceptional flavour. Described by Bunyard as "honeyed." Now seldom grown, but should do well as cordon, fuseau or bush in small garden.

Ribston Pippin. A medium to fairly large-sized, round to conical, apple, a dull greenish-yellow and brownish-red russet. Superb flavour, firm yellowish-white flesh, crisp, slightly dry and aromatic. Season, November to January. A moderately good cropper and stores well. Does best in sheltered situations and warm soil where ample moisture is available. Makes a moderate-sized standard, espalier, or bush, or may be grown as cordon; also useful for pot culture. One of the best desserts. Somewhat liable to canker and scab. Needs hard pruning. Self-sterile. (See Triploid varieties, page 191.) Needs diploid pollinator.

Rival. A medium to fairly large-sized, round, flattened and somewhat uneven-shaped apple, a beautiful salmon-carmine and rich yellow. Fair flavour, firm white flesh, crisp and juicy. Season, October to December. A fairly good cropper, keeping well into December. Makes a medium-sized, neat-growing standard or bush, pyramid or cordon. Of decorative value in the garden, recommended for pot culture, good for dessert, or cooking and also grown for market. The bad shape makes it difficult to pack in boxes. Said to be partially self-fertile. "Sulphur shy"—i.e., the leaf is susceptible to scorch when sprayed with lime-sulphur.

Rosemary Russet. A medium-sized, flattened, conical apple, yellow, flushed brick-red and russeted, with a very long, thin stalk. Good flavour, crisp yellowish flesh, juicy and aromatic. Season, December to March. A good cropper and stores well. Makes a moderate-sized standard or bush, or may be grown as espalier or cordon. Suitable for garden culture. One of the best late dessert russets. Self-sterile.

St. Cecilia. A medium-sized, oval apple, a beautiful golden-yellow, striped and flushed crimson. Fine flavour, sweet, juicy and rich. Season, January to March. A good cropper and stores well. Makes a weak, drooping bush. Not suitable for espalier or cordon. Recommended for private garden culture. Self-sterile. The leaf is susceptible to sulphur damage when sprayed.

St. Edmund's Russet. A small to medium-sized, round and flattened apple, an even, light golden russet all over. Excellent flavour, tender flesh, juicy and aromatic. Season, September to October. A good cropper but does not store and should be eaten as soon as possible after picking. Makes a moderately robust standard or bush. Too much of a tip-bearer for artificial forms. Said to be partially self-fertile. Much recommended as a small garden bush on Number IX stock.

St. Everard. A medium-sized, round-shaped apple, yellow and heavily striped with crimson. "Cox" flavour, tender, yellowish flesh, sweet and luscious. Season, August to September. A good cropper for *immediate* use and best eaten as soon as gathered. Forms a moderate-sized standard, or compact and sturdy bush and is one of the best early dessert apples and a good garden fruit, although a shy cropper. May also be grown as espalier or cordon. Said to be self-fertile. Susceptible to glassiness.

Sturmer Pippin. A small to medium-sized apple, a greenish-yellow with dull russet and rosy cheek. Good flavour, firm, greenish-white flesh, crisp, sweet and luscious. Season, March to May. A heavy cropper and stores well, provided it is not gathered too soon. Forms a compact standard or bush in almost any soil, or may be grown as espalier or cordon. A fine dessert apple. Said to be partially self-fertile. *Must have a warm, sunny situation to finish properly.*

Sunset. Medium, 2 1/2 × 1 1/2 inches, round, flattish apple; golden yellow with bright crimson flush. Stem long in a deep russeted cavity. Eye closed or part open in a shallow, slightly ribbed basin, sepals long. Flesh, yellowish, crisp and juicy, of very good flavour. Season, October to February. Tree vigorous and fertile. Leaves deep green. Mid-season flowering.

Wagener. A medium-sized, flattened, and somewhat irregular, round-shaped apple, yellow with bright crimson cheek. Good flavour, firm, yellowish flesh, juicy and tart. Season, April to June. A good cropper and storing well. Makes a compact-growing standard or bush. A good late cooker. Also used for dessert when fully ripe. Self-sterile.

Wealthy. A medium to fairly large-sized, beautiful round to conical apple, golden, striped and tinted with crimson or pale yellow. Nice flavour, soft and juicy. Season, October to December. A good cropper and keeps into December. Makes a compact-growing standard or bush, espalier or cordon. Useful alike for dessert or culinary purposes. Self-sterile.

White Transparent. Medium to large, round to conical, cooking or dessert. Season, mid-August. A Russian variety.

Winter Queening. Medium size, conical, yellow background almost covered with dark crimson. Handsome, good flavour, yellow flesh. Season December to March. Rather uncertain cropper.

Woolbrook Pippin. A new seedling of promise from Devonshire. A medium-sized round apple, red and yellow with some russet and a wide open eye. Season, after Christmas.

Worcester Pearmain. A medium-sized, round to conical apple, a bright crimson all over. Fair flavour, firm white flesh, crisp, luscious and aromatic. Season, September to early October. A good cropper and cold-stores well. Should not be gathered until well coloured and ripe. Does equally well in the colder districts and forms a medium-sized standard or bush. A good market apple and recommended for private garden culture. Said to be partially self-fertile. A tip-bearer and not suitable for artificial forms. Susceptible to scab and canker but one of the most regular cropping of all apples.

COOKING APPLES

Alfriston. A large-sized, round, flattened and irregular-shaped apple, greenish-yellow and russeted. Yellowish flesh, crisp, sharp and juicy. Delicious when cooked. Season, November to April. A good cropper and storing well provided the fruit is not picked before it is properly mature—early in November. Hardy even in the colder localities and grown in all forms, standard, espalier, bush or cordon. Self-sterile.

Annie Elizabeth. A medium to large-sized, round to conical and irregular-shaped apple, a glossy yellow, striped and splashed with bright scarlet. Crisp, white flesh, sharp and juicy. For cooking or dessert. Season, January to April. A good cropper when established. Makes a strong, upright standard or bush, or may be grown as espalier or cordon. Does well in the Midlands and Northern counties, and is an especial favourite in the Midlands and West Midlands. A good orchard apple. Said to be partially self-fertile. Late flowerer. Slow to come into bearing. Susceptible to scab and canker. Fruit very short on the stalk and apt to blow off. Susceptible to "scald" in store. Should be wrapped.

Arthur Turner. A new large-sized, round, green apple in season in August and September. Strong growing.

Barnack Beauty. See under Dessert Apples.

Bramley's Seedling. A large, flattened, round-shaped apple, green and sometimes tinted or flushed dull red. Fine flavour; firm, yellowish flesh, juicy and sharp. Season, November to March. A heavy cropper and stores well. Does well even in the colder Northern districts and on almost any soil, including heavy and dry soils, and forms a strong standard or bush. One of the best cooking apples. Too strong growing for small gardens or for cordon culture. Susceptible to scab, resistant to canker. Triploid variety, see page 191, and needs cross-pollinating diploid variety.

Crawley Beauty. A beautiful, large, even, round apple, green with red stripes. Good flavour, crisp, white flesh, juicy and tart. Season, March to April. A heavy cropper and stores well. Makes a fine standard or bush for garden culture. *Very late flowering.* Self-sterile.

Crimson Bramley. Similar in shape, size and other characteristics to the well-known Bramley's Seedling, which see, but coloured a bright crimson all over.

Early Victoria (Emneth Early). A medium-sized, conical apple, light green in colour. Good flavour, soft, white flesh, juicy and tart. Season, July to August. A heavy cropper but does not store and should be used as soon as possible. Market fruit should be picked before it is fully grown. Forms a fairly strong standard or bush and is one of the best early codlings for garden culture and market, thriving even in the colder localities. Needs severe fruit thinning. Said to be partially self-fertile. Responds well to spur-pruning.

Edward VII. A large, round to oblong apple, pale yellow with slight reddish-brown flush. Good flavour, firm flesh, juicy and sharp. Season, January to April. A shy cropper, storing well. Forms a strong-growing standard, bush or trained tree and is especially recommended for pyramid form. Good orchard or garden fruit. Late flowerer. Plant with Royal Jubilee, Crawley Beauty, or Court Pendu Plat for cross-pollination.

Emneth Early. See Early Victoria.

Encore. A very large flattened, round to oval apple, yellowish-green in colour and sometimes flushed and striped red. Fair flavour, tender, greenish flesh, juicy and acid. Season, November to June. A heavy cropper and keeps well in store. Forms a strong-growing standard or bush. Good orchard or garden fruit. Said to be partially self-fertile.

Grenadier. A large, flattened, round to conical apple, light green to pale yellow in colour. Good flavour, crisp, juicy and sharp. Season, end of July to October. A good cropper but does not store and should be used as soon after picking as possible. Makes a moderately strong-growing standard or bush and does well even in cold districts and on heavy soils. A popular market apple. A tip-bearer unsuitable for artificial forms. Prune lightly. Said to be partially self-fertile.

Lane's Prince Albert. A beautiful large, round to oval apple, light greenish-yellow, flushed and striped red. Good cooker, tender, white flesh, juicy and sharp. Season, November to April. A heavy cropper and storing well up to six months. A dwarf grower of pendulous habit best grown in bush or cordon form. Hardy even in the colder localities. This is one of the very best of all cooking apples for garden culture in any form. "Sulphur-shy."

Lord Derby. A very large, round to conical and irregular-shaped apple, dark green turning golden-yellow. Firm, yellowish flesh, juicy and sub-acid. Season, November to December. A good cropper and storing well to December. Does well in almost any soil, including heavy and cold land, and in the Midlands and Northern districts. Grown in all forms, standard, bush, espalier, or cordon. Recommended for private garden culture. Said to be partially self-fertile. Susceptible to brown rot.

Lord Grosvenor. A large, round to conical and irregular-shaped apple, a pale yellow turning whitish when ripe. Good flavour, tender, white flesh, juicy and sharp. Season, August to October. A heavy bearer but does not store and should be used as soon after picking as possible. Does well in all districts in almost any soil and may be grown in any form. Needs well thinning. Susceptible to scab. Said to be partially self-fertile.

Mank's Codlin. A conical apple of medium size, greenish-yellow with a slight red flush. Weak growth, but a heavy cropper. A cooking apple ripening in August. Has very beautiful large flowers.

Monarch (Seabrook's). A rather large, beautiful, roundish apple, light green with rosy flush. Good flavour, firm, white flesh, juicy and sub-acid. Season, October to April. A heavy cropper and storing well. Forms a vigorous and spreading standard or bush, or may be grown as espalier. Needs well thinning. Self-sterile.

Newton Wonder. A medium to large-sized, even and round-shaped apple, green to golden and beautifully tinged with red. Good flavour, crisp, yellowish-white flesh, juicy and acid. Season, October to April. A splendid cropper and stores well. A very strong grower. Does well almost anywhere, including the colder Northern districts, and forms a strong, spreading standard or bush. Late flowerer and slow to come into bearing. Too strong growing for cordon or small garden culture. One of the best late cookers and valuable for market or exhibition. Prune lightly. Said to be self-fertile.

Peasgood Nonsuch. A very large, even and round-shaped apple, a pale yellow and bright crimson. Good flavour, soft, yellowish flesh, juicy and acid. Season, October to November. A good cropper, but does not store and should be used as soon as possible after picking. Does well on light and chalky soils, where it makes a medium-sized standard or bush. In cold areas it does best trained on a wall. One of the best exhibition apples. Very subject to canker and brown rot. Self-sterile.

Rev. W. Wilks. A very large, flattened and ribbed, round-shaped apple, a pale yellow with red spots and slashes. Good flavour, tender, white flesh, juicy and sub-acid. Season, October to November. A good cropper but does not keep and should be used as soon as possible after picking. Of dwarf habit but hardy and usually grown as a bush in private gardens. Useful for exhibition. Subject to scab and brown rot. Said to be self-fertile.

Royal Jubilee. A large, beautiful round to conical apple, of clear golden hue. Good flavour, firm, yellowish flesh, juicy and sharp. Season, October to December. A good cropper and stores well. Does well even in the colder localities, forming a sturdy, flat-headed standard, bush or espalier. Recommended for garden culture. *Very late flowerer.* Self-sterile.

Seabrook's Monarch. See Monarch.

Stirling Castle. A medium to large-sized, even, flattened and round-shaped apple, yellow to green in colour. Good flavour, tender, whitish flesh, juicy and sharp. Season, September to October. A good cropper but does not keep and should be used as soon as possible after being picked. On light soil, even in the colder districts, makes a compact, dwarf-growing bush, espalier or cordon.

Should never be sprayed with lime-sulphur. Very prone to canker. Partially self-fertile.

Transparent de Croncels. A large-sized, round to oblong-shaped apple, a pale whitish-yellow, sometimes slightly flushed red. Good flavour, tender yellowish-white flesh, juicy and sub-acid. Season, October to December. A good cropper but does not keep long after picking. Makes a good standard or bush. Self-sterile.

Underleaf. A roundish apple of medium size, greenish-yellow, with slight russet on one side. Grown as a standard tree in grass orchards in the West Midlands, where it is considered one of the most reliable croppers. A cooking apple in season from November to February. *Very late flowerer.*

Wagener. See Dessert Apples.

Warner's King. A very large, flattened, round to conical apple, a pale yellow in colour. Good flavour, tender, whitish flesh, juicy and sub-acid. Season, November. A good cropper for immediate use. Does not like cold soils. Makes a large, spreading standard or bush, or may be grown in other forms. A good mid-season cooker for the orchard. Very prone to canker. Self-sterile. Triploid variety, see page 191.

Wellington. A medium-sized, flattened, even and round-shaped apple, pale yellow tinged red and russeted. Excellent flavour, crisp, whitish flesh, juicy and sharp. Season, December to March. A good cropper and stores well until March. Forms a moderately strong-growing standard or bush, or may be grown in other forms. Hardy even in the colder Northern localities, but highly susceptible to scab and canker. Self-sterile. Many experts consider it to be the best baking apple.

ORNAMENTAL AND FLOWERING CRAB APPLES

From the decorative point of view no fruit garden or

orchard is complete without its ornamental and flowering Crabs. The lovely soft and delicate blossoms are borne in early spring, while the highly-decorative fruits may be made into delicious preserve or jelly. Crabs require cultivation and treatment similar to that of the ordinary apple. Many varieties are highly susceptible to scab.

CRABS WITH DECORATIVE FLOWERS AND FRUIT

Dartmouth. Has beautiful, white-tinted flowers in early spring, followed by medium-sized, plum-shaped fruits with a purplish-red bloom. The fruit is very prolific and makes excellent preserve.

John Downie. Snowed under in early spring with a mass of lovely white flowers, followed by clusters of conical orange and scarlet fruits, which are very beautiful. A prolific bearer, but susceptible to scab.

Paul's Imperial Scarlet. Covered with lovely blossom in early spring, followed by a heavy crop of beautiful crimson miniature apples.

Siberian Scarlet. The masses of lovely blossom, borne in early spring, are followed by a prolific crop of cherry-like, bright scarlet fruits borne on longish stems. Excellent for preserve.

Transcendent. The beautiful and prolific blossom is followed by a heavy crop of very decorative golden-yellow fruits with rosy cheeks, borne on longish stems. This fruit has quite a good flavour.

Veitch's Scarlet. This is a cross between Siberian Scarlet Crab and King of the Pippins Apple. The lovely blossoms are followed by a prolific crop of ovate fruits, a rich crimson-scarlet over golden-yellow, with a pleasant sharp flavour.

CRABS TO GROW FOR DECORATION ALONE

Pyrus Malus aldenhamensis. An attractive tree, 8 to 12 feet or more in height, with masses of wine-coloured blossoms in spring and purple-red fruit in autumn.

Pyrus M. floribunda. The popular "Japanese Crab" is a very attractive tree, rather spreading in habit, reaching some 12 to 15 feet in height and nearly as much in diameter. In April and May it is smothered in lovely blossoms, which are crimson in bud, but open rosy-purple and as they become older turn pale pink to white. The fruit is of little account. *P. M. f. atrosanguinea* is a variety of the above with flowers of a somewhat deeper shade and turning to a rosy-pink.

Pyrus M. Eleyi. Is a beautiful tree 15 to 20 feet in height with vinous-red flowers, which open early and blend with the young, coppery foliage. The bunches of wine-red fruits are an added attraction in autumn.

Pyrus M. Lemoinei. Is a purple-flowering Crab even more intense in colouring than *P. M. Eleyi*, which it resembles in other respects.

Pyrus M. Neidzwetzkyana. The Manchurian Crab is

a conspicuous tree some 15 to 20 feet in height and with reddish-purple blossom and fruit. The foliage also assumes a purple hue as the season advances.

Pyrus Sargentii. A native of China, is a delightful, spreading bush, some 5 to 6 feet in height, with clusters of white blossoms, each individual flower being quite large. The fruits which follow are a brilliant scarlet. Budded on standard and half-standard crab stocks, this makes a graceful and attractive tree.

CIDER APPLES

There are three types of apple especially cultivated for the manufacture of cider and these are known as Bittersweets, Sweets and Sharps. All require cultivation and general treatment similar to that given to ordinary apples. Bittersweets are largely used in the production of good-class bottled cider. Sweets, being of a milder flavour and possessing more sugar, are useful for blending purposes; and Sharps also are useful for blending. No one should attempt planting cider apples without first consulting the National Fruit and Cider Institute, Long Ashton, Bristol, or his county advisory officer.

Bittersweets

Belle Norman. An early variety.

Chisel Jersey. A useful late variety, recommended by the National Fruit and Cider Institute, Long Ashton, Bristol. A good cropper.

Cummy Norman. A mid-season variety.

Dabinett. An excellent cider apple recommended by the Ministry of Agriculture, and the Midland Cider Makers' Association. A good and early cropper. Ready in October.

Eggleton Styre. Can be used without blending. (Mid-season.)

Knotted Kernel. A high-grade crimson cider apple recommended by the Ministry of Agriculture, and the Midland Cider Makers' Association. A regular and heavy cropper, ready in October.

Major. A favourite cider apple with the Devonshire Manufacturers. Early and prolific and recommended by the Ministry of Agriculture.

Royal Wilding. A useful blending apple ready November to December. Recommended by the Ministry of Agriculture, and the Midland Cider Makers' Association. A medium cropper.

Strawberry Norman. A fine-class cider apple, recommended by the Ministry of Agriculture, and the Gloucestershire Agricultural Department. A good cropper, ready October to November.

White Close Pippin. A useful blending apple ready in November. Recommended by the National Fruit and Cider Institute, Bristol. Also useful for jam-making.

Sweets

Killerton Sweet. An early variety.

Slack ma Girdle. An excellent late sweet apple, recommended by the Ministry of Agriculture, and the Midland Cider Makers' Association, and a favourite variety with the Devonshire manufacturers. A good cropper, ready November to December. Also good for jam-making.

Sweet Alford. A highly-recommended cider apple and a favourite in all quarters. Crops well and ready in mid-season (November). Also useful for jam-making.

Sweet Coppin. Another good sweet variety, recommended by the Midland Cider Makers' Association, and the Gloucestershire Agricultural Department. Rich flavour and regular cropper. Ready in October.

White Jersey. A good early sweet apple, recommended by the National Fruit and Cider Institute, Long Ashton, Bristol. A fine and regular cropper. Ready October.

Sharps

Blackwell Red. An early variety.

Cap of Liberty. Also known as Bloody Butcher and Red Soldier. An excellent vintage cider apple, recommended by the Ministry of Agriculture, and the Midland Cider Makers' Association. A good and regular cropper. Ready November. Prefers a heavy soil of the limestone formation.

Crimson King. Another fine mid-season cider apple.

Dymock Red. A mid-season variety.

Foxwhelp. A splendid vintage cider apple, highly recommended by the Ministry of Agriculture, and the Midland Cider Makers' Association. Regular cropper. Ready November.

Kingston Black. Another highly-recommended and much-prized variety. Excellent cropper and ready in November. Susceptible to canker and with definite soil preferences. Can be used without blending.

New Foxwhelp. A mid-season variety.

Ponsford. A late variety recommended by the National Fruit and Cider Institute, Long Ashton, Bristol. Crops well and stores December to April. Also useful for jam-making.

Reinette Obry. Another very highly-prized late cider apple, recommended for all parts. A strong cropper, ready November to December. Also useful for jam-making.

NOTE ON IDENTIFICATION OF VARIETIES

The foregoing notes make no pretence to give a full description of the hundreds of varieties of apples that exist in this country. For this purpose two books of reference are available, which, studied together, should enable the reader to identify any but the most obscure local varieties. These books are E. A. Bunyard's "Handbook of Fruits," Apples and Pears, and H. V. Taylor's "The Apples of England."

When sending apples or other fruits to experts for

identification, it is very important to send at least two typical specimens of the fruit, together with specimens of the current year's shoot growth and as full a description as possible of the age and growth habit of the tree and of the conditions under which it is being grown.

The specimens should be packed in such a way as to ensure that they arrive in a fresh condition.

EARLY-BLOSSOMING VARIETIES OF APPLE

Beauty of Bath (D)

Belle de Boskoop (D)

Duchess's Favourite (D)

Egremont Russet (D)

Gravenstein (D)

Irish Peach (D)

Langley Pippin (D)

Mank's Codling (C)

Mr. Gladstone (D)

Oslin (C)

Rev. W. Wilks (C)

Ribston Pippin (D)

St. Edmund's Russet (D)

Wagener (D)

LATE BLOSSOMING VARIETIES

American Mother (D)

Annie Elizabeth (C)

Christmas Pearmain (D)

Edward VII (C)

Heusgen's Golden Reinette (D)

Transparent de Croncels (C)

White Transparent (C)

VERY LATE BLOSSOMING VARIETIES

Court Pendu Plat (D)   Royal Jubilee (C)

Crawley Beauty (C)   Underleaf (C)

C = Cooking; D = Dessert.

A certain limited number of apple varieties will set a fair to good percentage of their blossom in most seasons when planted entirely alone. In spite of this the wisest course is never to plant a single variety in any quantity without making sure that some other variety with a similar blossoming period is planted within easy flying distance of bees and other insects as a "pollinator."

When planting any of the varieties given in the above lists of early and late blossomers, care should be taken to see that the pollinator variety belongs to the same group of blossoming period. As to varieties not included in these lists, there should be no difficulty, as these should usually cross-pollinate.

TRIPLOID VARIETIES OF APPLE

Belle de Boskoop (D)   Gravenstein (D)

Blenheim Orange (D)   Ribston Pippin (D)

Bramley's Seedling (C)   Warner's King (C)

C = Cooking; D = Dessert.

Recent research into the cytology of the apple by M. B. Crane and his fellow-workers at the John Innes Horticultural

Institution at Merton has revealed an important difference in the genetical make-up of a small group of apple varieties, a difference in the number of chromosomes or "carriers of the hereditary factors." The majority of apple varieties are "diploids" and have 34 chromosomes, but this small group of "triploids" have 51 chromosomes.*

Crane's experiments in cross-pollinating varieties of these two groups showed that the triploid varieties would not cross-pollinate each other at all well, and were not very good cross-pollinators even for the vast majority of diploid varieties.

In the light of present knowledge, therefore, it would be clearly unwise to plant up an orchard of triploid varieties only or to use them as pollinators for each other. For the commercial grower it would also seem important, when planting *Bramley's Seedling*, to include at least two other varieties, both diploids, to ensure efficient cross-pollination of the *Bramley's Seedling* and of each other.

APPLES SPECIALLY RECOMMENDED FOR
GARDEN PLANTING

Dessert

Adam's Pearmain	Heusgen's Golden Reinette	Laxton's Superb
American Mother	Irish Peach	May Queen
Claygate Pearmain	James Grieve	Miller's Seedling
Christmas Pearmain	King's Acre Pippin	Orleans Reinette
Cornish Gillyflower	Laxton's Advance	Pitmaston Pine Apple
Cox's Orange Pippin	Laxton's Epicure	Rosemary Russet
D'Arcy Spice	Laxton's Exquisite	St. Edmund's Russet
Duke of Devonshire	Laxton's Fortune	St. Everard
Egremont Russet		Sturmer Pippin

Cookers

Arthur Turner	Encore	Monarch
Bramley's Seedling	Grenadier	Peasgood Nonsuch
Crawley Beauty	Lane's Prince Albert	Rev. W. Wilks
Early Victoria	Lord Derby	Royal Jubilee
Edward VII	Lord Grosvenor	Stirling Castle

DESSERT APPLES FOR GROWING ON WEST WALLS

Claygate Pearmain	Laxton's Exquisite	Ribston Pippin
Cox's Orange Pippin	Orleans Reinette	Rosemary Russet
King's Acre Pippin	Pitmaston Pine Apple	Sturmer Pippin

ORDER OF RIPENING OF SOME GOOD VARIETIES

Early (July–September)

Variety	Garden or Orchard	Dessert or Cooking
Arthur Turner	Garden	Cooking (*Immediate use*)
Early Victoria	Garden or Orchard	Cooking (*Immediate use*)
Irish Peach	Garden	Dessert (*Immediate use*)
Lady Sudeley	Garden or Orchard	Dessert (*Immediate use*)
Grenadier	Garden or Orchard	Cooking (*Immediate use*)
Miller's Seedling	Garden	Dessert (*Immediate use*)
Mr. Gladstone	Garden or Orchard	Dessert (*Immediate use*)
Devonshire Quarrenden	Garden or Orchard	Dessert (*Immediate use*)
Laxton's Advance	Garden	Dessert (*Immediate use*)
Laxton's Epicure	Garden	Dessert (*Immediate use*)

Mid-Season (September–November)

Variety	Garden or Orchard	Dessert or Cooking
American Mother	Garden or Orchard	Dessert
Charles Ross	Garden	Dessert and Cooking
Egremont Russet	Garden	Dessert
Ellison's Orange	Garden or Orchard	Dessert. (*Immediate use*)
Golden Noble	Garden	Cooking (*Stores well*)
James Grieve	Garden	Dessert (*Immediate use*)
King of the Pippins	Garden or Orchard	Dessert (*Keeps well*)
Laxton's Exquisite	Garden	Dessert (*Immediate use*)
Laxton's Fortune	Garden or Orchard	Dessert (*Immediate use*)
Lord Derby	Garden or Orchard	Cooking (*Keeps to Decembe*
Peasgood Nonsuch	Garden or Orchard	Dessert and Cooking
Rev. W. Wilks	Garden	Cooking (*Immediate use*)
Rival	Garden or Orchard	Dessert (*Stores well*)
Worcester Pearmain	Garden or Orchard	Dessert (*Immediate use*)

Ripening Late (November–March)

Variety	Garden or Orchard	Dessert or Cooking
Adam's Pearmain	Garden	Dessert
Annie Elizabeth	Garden or Orchard	Cooking and Dessert
Belle de Boskoop	Orchard	Dessert and Cooking
Blenheim Orange	Orchard	Dessert and Cooking
Bramley's Seedling	Orchard	Cooking
Cox's Orange Pippin	Garden or Orchard	Dessert
Lane's Prince Albert	Garden or Orchard	Cooking
Laxton's Superb	Garden or Orchard	Dessert
Monarch	Garden or Orchard	Cooking
Newton Wonder	Orchard	Cooking
King's Acre Pippin	Garden or Orchard	Dessert
Orleans Reinette	Garden or Orchard	Dessert
Ribston Pippin	Garden or Orchard	Dessert
St. Cecilia	Garden	Dessert
Sturmer Pippin	Garden	Dessert

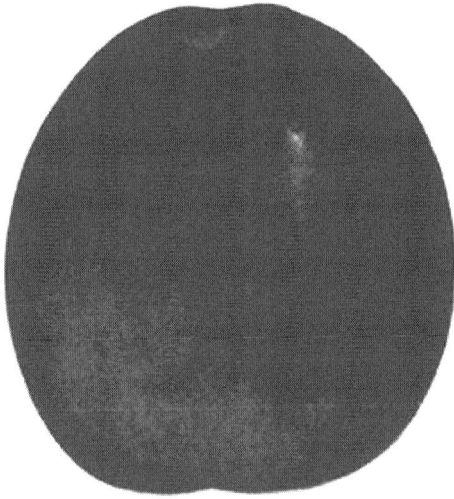

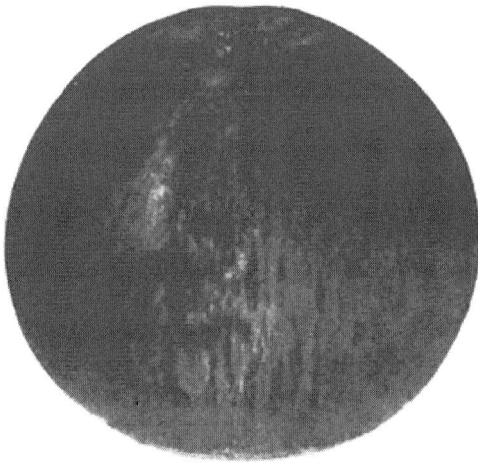

APPLES—*Belle de Boskoop* (*top*) and *Cox's Orange Pippin* (*bottom*)

SELECTION OF GOOD COMMERCIAL VARIETIES

Bramley's Seedling (C)	Grenadier (C)	Miller's Seedling (D)
Cox's Orange Pippin (D)	James Grieve (D)	Newton Wonder (C)
Early Victoria (C)	Laxton's Superb (D)	Worcester Pearmain (D)
Ellison's Orange (D)	Lord Derby (C)	

SCAB RESISTANT VARIETIES

Variety	Garden or Orchard	Dessert or Cooking
Belle de Boskoop	Garden or Orchard	Dessert or Cooking
Charles Ross	Garden	Dessert
Court Pendu Plat	Garden or Orchard	Dessert
Duke of Devonshire	Garden or Orchard	Dessert
Early Victoria	Garden or Orchard	Cooking
Grenadier	Garden or Orchard	Cooking
Egremont Russet	Garden	Dessert
King Edward VII	Garden or Orchard	Cooking
Northern Greening	Orchard	Cooking
Wyken Pippin	Garden or Orchard	Dessert

ESPECIALLY HARDY SORTS

Variety	Garden or Orchard	Dessert or Cooking
Alfriston	Garden or Orchard	Cooking
Allington Pippin	Garden or Orchard	Dessert
Beauty of Bath	Garden or Orchard	Dessert
Bramley's Seedling	Garden or Orchard	Cooking
Devonshire Quarrenden	Garden or Orchard	Dessert
Early Victoria	Garden or Orchard	Cooking
Grenadier	Garden or Orchard	Cooking
James Grieve	Garden or Orchard	Dessert
Lady Sudeley	Garden or Orchard	Dessert
Lane's Prince Albert	Garden	Cooking
Mr. Gladstone	Garden or Orchard	Dessert
Newton Wonder	Orchard	Cooking

106

VARIETIES FOR GROWING IN POTS

Variety	Early or Late	Dessert or Cooking
Calville Blanche	Late	Dessert
Charles Ross	Mid-season	Dessert
Cox's Orange Pippin	Mid-season	Dessert
Ellison's Orange	Mid-season	Dessert
Irish Peach	Early	Dessert
James Grieve	Early	Dessert
Lady Sudeley	Mid-season	Dessert
Laxton's Exquisite	Mid-season	Dessert
Laxton's Fortune	Mid-season	Dessert
Laxton's Premier	Early	Dessert
Melba	Early	Dessert
Miller's Seedling	Mid-season	Dessert
Patricia	Mid-season	Dessert
Peasgood Nonsuch	Mid-season	Cooking
Rev. W. Wilks	Mid-season	Cooking
Wealthy	Late	Dessert
White Transparent	Early	Dessert or Cooking

VARIETIES FOR EXHIBITION AT AMATEUR SHOWS

Variety	Garden or Orchard	Dessert or Cooking
Bramley's Seedling	Garden or Orchard	Cooking
Charles Eyre	Orchard	Cooking
Charles Ross	Garden	Dessert
Cox's Orange Pippin	Garden or Orchard	Dessert
Ellison's Orange	Garden or Orchard	Dessert
Fortune	Garden	Dessert
John Standish	Garden or Orchard	Dessert
Laxton's Superb	Garden or Orchard	Dessert
Newton Wonder	Orchard	Cooking
Peasgood Nonsuch	Garden or Orchard	Cooking
Rev. W. Wilks	Garden or Orchard	Cooking
Rival	Garden or Orchard	Dessert
Wealthy	Garden or Orchard	Dessert
Worcester Pearmain	Garden or Orchard	Dessert

107

BEST-FLAVOURED APPLES

Dessert

Variety	Garden or Orchard	Season of Best Flavour
Adam's Pearmain	Garden	December–March
Blenheim Orange	Orchard	December
Brownlees Russet	Garden	December–March
Claygate Pearmain	Garden	December–March
Cornish Gillyflower	Orchard	December–March
Cox's Orange Pippin	Garden	December
D'Arcy Spice	Garden or Orchard	February–May
Egremont Russet	Garden	October
Irish Peach	Garden	September
James Grieve	Garden or Orchard	September
King's Acre Pippin	Garden	February
Laxton's Exquisite	Garden	September
Laxton's Superb	Garden or Orchard	January–March
Mother (American)	Garden or Orchard	End of October
Orleans Reinette	Garden or Orchard	December–March
Owen Thomas	Garden	August
Pitmaston Pine Apple	Garden	March
Ribston Pippin	Garden or Orchard	November
Rosemary Russet	Garden	February
St. Edmund's Russet	Garden	September
St. Everard	Garden	September

Cookers

Variety	Garden or Orchard	Best time to Cook
Annie Elizabeth	Garden or Orchard	January–February
Bramley's Seedling	Garden or Orchard	January–February
Edward VII	Garden or Orchard	February–March
Grenadier	Garden or Orchard	August
Lane's Prince Albert	Garden	October–November
Newton Wonder	Garden or Orchard	February–March
Rev. W. Wilks	Garden or Orchard	September–October
Stirling Castle	Garden or Orchard	September
Wellington	Garden or Orchard	March

Note.—Those readers who are interested in the best-flavoured varieties of fruits should not fail to read "The Anatomy of Dessert," by E. A. Bunyard.

SELECTION OF VERY LARGE VARIETIES

Variety	Garden or Orchard	Dessert or Cooking
Beauty of Kent	Garden or Orchard	Cooking
Bramley's Seedling	Garden or Orchard	Cooking
Charles Eyre	Garden	Cooking
Charles Ross	Garden	Dessert
Gascoyne's Scarlet	Orchard	Dessert or Cooking
Gloria Mundi	Garden	Cooking
King of Tompkin's County	Orchard, Pot or Garden	Dessert
Lane's Prince Albert	Garden	Cooking
Lord Derby	Garden or Orchard	Cooking
Mère de Ménage	Garden or Orchard	Cooking
Newton Wonder	Orchard	Cooking
Peacemaker	Garden or Orchard	Dessert
Peasgood Nonsuch	Garden	Cooking
Rev. W. Wilks	Garden	Cooking

VARIETIES SUITABLE FOR PARTICULAR FORMS

Standards or Half-Standards

Plant 30 to 40 feet apart, according to Variety and Soil

Variety	Stock	Dessert or Cooking
American Mother	East Malling XVI or Selected Crab	Dessert
Beauty of Bath	East Malling XVI or Selected Crab	Dessert
Belle de Boskoop	East Malling XVI or Selected Crab	Dessert
Blenheim Orange	East Malling XVI or Selected Crab	Dessert
Bramley's Seedling	East Malling XVI or Selected Crab	Cooking
Crawley Beauty	East Malling XVI or Selected Crab	Cooking
Duke of Devonshire	East Malling XVI or Selected Crab	Dessert
Edward VII	East Malling XVI or Selected Crab	Cooking
Grenadier	East Malling XVI or Selected Crab	Cooking
Laxton's Superb	East Malling XVI or Selected Crab	Dessert
Monarch	East Malling XVI or Selected Crab	Cooking
Orleans Reinette	East Malling XVI or Selected Crab	Dessert

Bushes

Plant 10 to 30 feet apart, according to Stock, Soil and
Variety

Variety	Stock	Dessert or Cooking
Adam's Pearmain	East Malling IX, II, I or XVI	Dessert
Barnack Beauty	East Malling IX, II, I or XVI	Dessert
Bramley's Seedling	East Malling IX, II, I or XVI	Cooking
Charles Ross	East Malling IX, II, I or XVI	Dessert
Cornish Gillyflower	East Malling IX, II, I or XVI	Dessert
Cox's Orange Pippin	East Malling IX, II, I or XVI	Dessert
Egremont Russet	East Malling IX, II, I or XVI	Dessert
Ellison's Orange	East Malling IX, II, I or XVI	Dessert
Gladstone	East Malling II, I or XVI	Dessert
Grenadier	East Malling II, I or XVI	Cooking
Irish Peach	East Malling II, I or XVI	Dessert
Langley's Pippin	East Malling II, I or XVI	Dessert
Lord Lambourne	East Malling IX, II, I or XVI	Dessert
Orleans Reinette	East Malling IX, II, I or XVI	Dessert
Owen Thomas	East Malling II, I or XVI	Dessert
St. Cecilia	East Malling IX, II, I or XVI	Dessert
Worcester Pearmain	East Malling IX, II, I or XVI	Dessert

VARIETIES SUITABLE FOR GROWING AS DWARF PYRAMID AND CORDON

Plant Single-vertical or oblique cordon 2 to 3 feet
apart,

Single-horizontal cordon 10 to 12 feet apart,

Double-U cordon 5 to 6 feet apart, and

Dwarf Pyramid 3 to 6 feet apart.

Variety	Stock	Dessert or Cooking
American Mother	East Malling IX, II or I	Dessert
Cox's Orange Pippin	East Malling IX, II or I	Dessert
Early Victoria	East Malling IX, II or I	Cooking
Edward VII	East Malling IX, II or I	Cooking
Egremont Russet	East Malling IX, II or I	Dessert
Ellison's Orange	East Malling IX, II or I	Dessert
James Grieve	East Malling II or I	Dessert
Lane's Prince Albert	East Malling IX, II or I	Cooking
Laxton's Fortune	East Malling IX, II or I	Dessert
Laxton's Superb	East Malling IX	Dessert
Lord Lambourne	East Malling IX, II or I	Dessert
Miller's Seedling	East Malling II or I	Dessert
Ribston Pippin	East Malling IX, II or I	Dessert
St. Cecilia	East Malling IX, II or I	Dessert

ESPALIERS

Plant about 15 to 20 feet apart.

Variety	Stock	Dessert or Cooking
American Mother	East Malling IX, II or I	Dessert
Belle de Boskoop	East Malling IX	Dessert
Blenheim Orange	East Malling IX	Dessert
Brownlees Russet	East Malling IX, II or I	Dessert
Cox's Orange Pippin	East Malling IX, II or I	Dessert
Crawley Beauty	East Malling II or I	Cooking
Early Victoria	East Malling II or I	Cooking
Edward VII	East Malling IX, II or I	Cooking
Egremont Russet	East Malling II or I	Dessert
James Grieve	East Malling II, I or XVI	Dessert
King's Acre Pippin	East Malling II, I or XVI	Dessert
Lane's Prince Albert	East Malling II, I or XVI	Cooking
Laxton's Superb	East Malling IX	Dessert
Lord Lambourne	East Malling IX, II or I	Dessert
Ribston Pippin	East Malling IX, II or I	Dessert

BEST ORCHARD VARIETIES

111

Variety	Season	Dessert or Cooking
Beauty of Bath	Early August	Dessert
Belle de Boskoop	Late (Dec.–March)	Dessert or Cooking
Blenheim Orange	Late (Nov.–January)	Dessert or Cooking
Bramley's Seedling	Late (Nov.–March)	Cooking
Duke of Devonshire	Late (March–April)	Dessert
Laxton's Superb	Late (Nov.–February)	Dessert
Lord Derby	Late (Nov.–December)	Cooking
Monarch	Late (Dec.–March)	Cooking
Newton Wonder	Late (Feb.–March)	Cooking
Ribston Pippin	Late (Nov.–January)	Dessert

*This work is lucidly dealt with in "The Apple," by Sir Daniel Hall and M. B. Crane, published in 1933; see also "The Fertility Rules in Fruit Planting," John Innes Leaflet No. 4, published by the John Innes Horticultural institution, London, S.W. 19.

27952358R00070

Printed in Great Britain
by Amazon